I0447022

United States
Department of
Agriculture

Forest Service

Pacific Southwest
Research Station

General Technical Report
PSW-GTR-236

December 2011

A Risk Assessment of Climate Change and the Impact of Forest Diseases on Forest Ecosystems in the Western United States and Canada

John T. Kliejunas

The **Forest Service** of the U.S. Department of Agriculture is dedicated to the principle of multiple use management of the Nation's forest resources for sustained yields of wood, water, forage, wildlife, and recreation. Through forestry research, cooperation with the States and private forest owners, and management of the National Forests and National Grasslands, it strives—as directed by Congress—to provide increasingly greater service to a growing Nation.

Author

John T. Kliejunas was a regional forest pathologist (retired), U.S. Department of Agriculture, Forest Service, Pacific Southwest Region, Vallejo, CA.

Cover photographs (clockwise from upper left): Armillaria root disease, by Michael Cruickshank, Natural Resources Canada; Dothistroma needle blight, by David Weaver, British Columbia Forest Service; yellow-cedar decline, by Paul Hennon, USDA Forest Service, Pacific Northwest Research Station; sudden oak death, by Marin Municipal Water District; white pine blister rust, by Detlev Vogler, USDA Forest Service, Pacific Southwest Research Station; dwarf mistletoe infection, by Paul Hennon, USDA Forest Service, Pacific Northwest Research Station.

Abstract

Kliejunas, John T. 2011. A risk assessment of climate change and the impact of forest diseases on forest ecosystems in the Western United States and Canada. Gen. Tech. Rep. PSW-GTR-236. Albany, CA: U.S. Department of Agriculture, Forest Service, Pacific Southwest Research Station. 70 p.

This risk assessment projects the effects of eight forest diseases under two climate-change scenarios (warmer and drier, warmer and wetter). Examples are used to describe how various types of forest diseases may respond to environmental changes. Forest diseases discussed in this report include foliar diseases, *Phytophthora* diseases, stem rusts, canker diseases, dwarf mistletoes, root diseases, and yellow-cedar decline. The likelihood and consequences of increased damage to forests from each disease as a result of climate change are analyzed and assigned a risk value of high, moderate, or low. The risk value is based on available biological information and subjective judgment. Although results suggest that climate change will affect forest health, uncertainty arises regarding the degree of climate change that will occur; pathogen biology under changing climate; the effects of changing climate directly on the host; and the interactions between the pathogen, host, and climate.

Keywords: Climate change, forest pathogens, environmental risk assessment, foliar diseases, *Phytophthora*, *Armillaria*, stem rusts, canker diseases, dwarf mistletoe, root diseases, yellow-cedar decline.

Summary

This risk assessment projects the effects of eight forest diseases under two climate-change scenarios (warmer and drier, warmer and wetter). Examples are used to describe how various types of forest diseases may respond to environmental changes. The likelihood and consequences of increased damage to forests from each disease as a result of climate change are analyzed and assigned a risk value of high, moderate, or low. The risk value is based on available biological information and subjective judgment.

Foliar diseases. Because most foliar pathogens require moisture for sporulation, dissemination, and infection, decreases in precipitation generally will lessen the likelihood of disease damage. Some needle cast diseases caused by species of *Davisomycella* and *Hypodermella* also require moisture for sporulation, dispersal, and infection, but are more likely to infect trees that are stressed by drought.

***Phytophthora* diseases.** Increased precipitation during spring is likely to be associated with increased prevalence of *Phytophthora ramorum* in areas where it already occurs and expansion of the pathogen to new locations. Continued warming would increase areas suitable climatically for *Phytophthora* species, resulting in increased tree mortality if the pathogen is introduced to those areas. However, moisture must be sufficient for pathogen sporulation and infection.

Stem rusts. The biology of stem rust pathogens on two-needled and three-needle pines in western North America—for example, western gall rust (*Endocronartium harknessii*), comandra rust (*Cronartium comandrae*), stalactiform rust (*C. coleosporioides*), and sweet fern rust (*C. comptoniae*)—is similar to white pine blister rust (*C. ribicola*). Infection and incidence of diseases caused by these fungi generally increase when conditions are cool and moist. Warmer conditions, whether wetter or drier, would be less favorable than cooler conditions.

Canker diseases. Most canker diseases are caused by facultative parasites such as *Botryosphaeria*, *Sphaeropsis*, *Cytospora*, and *Biscogniauxia* (*Hypoxylon*). We describe the risk potentials for *Cytospora* canker of alder, which can be extrapolated to other stress-related canker diseases. These fungi are more likely to cause damage to trees that are stressed by heat and drought. Not all canker diseases are associated with stressed hosts. The incidence of some canker pathogens, such as *Thyronectria austro-americana* on honeylocust (*Gleditsia triacanthos* L.) and *Cryphonectria cubensis* on *Eucalyptus* spp. L'Her., is associated with high rainfall, and their hosts display some resistance to drought stress.

Dwarf mistletoes. Warmer temperatures may enable range expansion of some dwarf mistletoes. An increased incidence of summer drought would increase mortality of infected trees.

Root diseases. A warmer climate will generally increase *Armillaria* incidence and impact as host stress increases. A drier climate would, in general, stress hosts more than a wetter climate, and thus increase host susceptibility to root diseases.

Yellow-cedar decline. Continued warming would likely increase mortality of yellow-cedar (*Chamaecyparis nootkatensis* (D. Don) Spach). The resulting economic and environmental loss rates are potentially high, but would depend on whether the trees are salvaged for value.

Although the results of this risk assessment suggest that climate change will affect forest health, the uncertainties associated with the risk potentials should be kept in mind. In this assessment, uncertainty arises regarding the degree of climate change that will occur; pathogen biology under changing climate; the effects of changing climate directly on the host; and the interactions between the pathogen, host, and climate.

The information provided in this risk assessment is directed to decisionmakers and managers for strategic and management planning. This risk assessment also serves as the basis for subsequent products—such as fact sheets, press releases, presentations, or decision documents—for nontechnical audiences.

Contents

Introduction

The objectives of this risk assessment are to estimate the likelihood that forest diseases will cause increased damage to forest ecosystems as a direct result of projected climate change by 2100, and to describe the potential economic and environmental consequences of that damage.

Risk Assessment Process

Risk analysis is a formal process that includes three successive steps: risk assessment, risk management, and risk communication (FAO and WHO 1995). A framework to guide risk assessments (NRC 1983) has been broadly adopted by national and international agencies.

An ecological risk assessment is defined as a process that evaluates the likelihood and associated uncertainty that adverse ecological effects may occur or are occurring as a result of exposure to one or more stressors (EPA 1992). An ecological risk assessment organizes and analyzes data, information, assumptions, and uncertainties to evaluate the likelihood and consequences of adverse ecological effects. Basically, it is a process used to determine what can happen, what the likelihood of the occurrence is, what the consequences are, and how certain the knowledge is. The purpose of conducting an ecological risk assessment is to provide decisionmakers with scientific information and other factors they need to consider (e.g., social, legal, political, or economic) in selecting a course of action.

An ecological risk assessment includes three primary phases: problem formulation, analysis, and risk characterization. In the first phase, which also may be referred to as hazard identification, the problem (source of potential adverse effects) is stated and described and a plan for analysis is developed. Two activities are conducted during the analysis phase: characterization or assessment of the probability of exposure and characterization or assessment of ecological effects (i.e., consequences of exposure). During the risk characterization phase, ecological risks (risk potentials) are estimated, the level of uncertainty in the risk estimates is specified, and evidence supporting the risk estimates is cited.

In this ecological risk assessment, I estimate the likelihood that projected changes in climate by 2100 (the exposure) and associated responses of biotic and abiotic tree pathogens (the threats or hazards) will adversely affect forests.

Problem formulation—

Recent literature reviews (Boland and others 2004, Desprez-Loustau and others 2007, Dukes and others 2009, Kliejunas and others 2009, Klopfenstein and others 2009a, Moore and Allard 2008, Sturrock 2007, Sturrock and others 2011, Woods and others 2010) suggest that projected changes in climate will increase damage to forests from pathogens.

A broad range of taxonomic groups and modes of infection of pathogens were considered for individual risk assessments. First, pathogens were classified by type of disease caused (e.g., foliar diseases, branch or bole diseases, root diseases). It was assumed that a risk assessment for one pathogen in a given class likely would be transferable to other pathogens in the class. Second, pathogens for which responses to weather or climate are documented in the research literature were identified. By necessity, risk assessments focus on those organisms for which biological information is available. Individual risk assessments were then conducted for two foliar pathogens (Dothistroma needle blight and Swiss needle cast), an aerial *Phytophthora* (sudden oak death/ramorum blight), a rust disease (white pine blister rust), a canker disease (Cytospora canker of alder), dwarf mistletoes, a root disease (Armillaria root disease), and an abiotic disease (yellow-cedar decline).

Analysis—

In this climate change risk assessment, I analyzed the likelihood and consequences of increased damage to forests from each disease as a result of climate change.

The likelihood and the consequences of increased disease damage were assigned a risk value of high, moderate, or low. A risk value is based on available biological information and subjective judgment. The criteria used to determine risk values were based on those developed by the U.S. Department of Agriculture Forest Service's Wood Import Pest Risk Assessment Mitigation and Evaluation Team (WIPRAMET) (Kliejunas and others 2003) and used by the U.S. Department of Agriculture Forest Service's Exotic Forest Pest Information System for North America (ExFor) (Downing and O'Brien 2004). The criteria estimate the effects of climate change on host susceptibility to the pathogen and on the ability of the pathogen to reproduce, spread, and infect the host. Professional judgment is required to assign a risk value when information is unavailable or different sources of information conflict. Therefore, the likelihood and the consequences were each assigned a certainty category as described in Orr and others (1993). The certainty categories are a function of the information that is available and the confidence of the assessor in it. Certainty categories used in the risk assessment process are:

- Very certain
- Reasonably certain
- Moderately certain
- Reasonably uncertain
- Very uncertain

Projected changes in climate vary by geographical region. In general, temperature is projected to increase. In different regions, and sometimes in different climate models for the same region, precipitation is projected to remain constant, decrease, or increase.

Temperature and moisture strongly affect pathogens and disease development by shaping survival, reproductive rate, and, in many cases, the probability of spread at a regional or larger scale. Two general scenarios of climate change were considered: warmer and drier, and warmer and wetter.

Likelihood of increased disease damage—

Five criteria were used to estimate likelihood (risk) of increased disease damage:

a. Suitability of conditions for pathogen survival, reproduction, spread, or host infection will increase as climate changes.

b. Changes in climate will stress the host and increase its susceptibility to the pathogen.

c. Pathogen is capable of substantial increases in population size (has a high reproductive potential).

d. Pathogen has a broad host range.

e. Control techniques are unknown, not feasible, or ineffective.

Criteria a and b are based on the direct effects of climate change on stages of the disease cycle (survival, reproduction, spread, infection) or on the effects of climate change on host stress. Factors considered included effect of milder winters on pathogen survival; effects of temperature and moisture (increase or decrease) on reproduction rates, infection, disease progress, and on subsequent success of pathogen; and effect on host stress. Criteria c, d, and e relate to the attributes of the disease or pathogen regardless of climate. For example, if the pathogen has a low reproductive potential or its host has a limited range, the likelihood of an increase in disease damage always will be low.

Using the above criteria, high, moderate, or low risk was assigned as follows:

High risk = Criteria a or b applies, and three or more of the remaining criteria a or b, c, d, and e apply.

Moderate risk = Criteria a or b applies, and two or fewer of the remaining criteria a or b, c, d, and e apply.

Low risk = Criteria a and b do not apply, and one or more of criteria c, d, and e apply.

Consequences of increased disease damage—
Five criteria—based on the economic and environmental effects of increased disease, regardless of change in climate—were used to categorize the potential economic or environmental consequences of increased disease damage.

a. Hosts of pathogen have substantial commercial value.
b. Pathogen directly causes host mortality or increases the probability that other organisms will kill the host.
c. Damage caused by pathogen decreases economic value of the host.
d. Pathogen causes substantial direct environmental effects, such as extensive ecological disruption or reduction in species richness over extensive areas.
e. Pathogen affects a host or hosts with limited natural distribution.

Risk was assigned as follows:

High risk = Three or more of the five criteria apply.

Moderate risk = Two of the five criteria apply.

Low risk = One or none of the five criteria apply.

Risk characterization (estimate of risk potential)—
The risk potential resulting from climate change was estimated as the likelihood of increased disease damage multiplied by the potential consequences of increased disease damage. The risk potential for each disease was estimated using a method developed by Orr and others (1993). The method has been used by WIPRAMET and quantified by ExFor by assigning integer values of 3, 2, and 1 to risk classes high, moderate, and low, respectively (table 1).

Table 1—Classes and values of risk potential

Likelihood of increased disease damage	Consequences of increased disease damage	Risk potential
High (3)	High (3)	Very high (9)
Medium (2)	High (3)	High (6)
Low (1)	High (3)	Medium (3)
High (3)	Medium (2)	High (6)
Medium (2)	Medium (2)	Medium (4)
Low (1)	Medium (2)	Low (2)
High (3)	Low (1)	Medium (3)
Medium (2)	Low (1)	Low (2)
Low (1)	Low (1)	Very low (1)

Climate Change and Forest Pathogens

Climate Projections

Global—

Climate change often is projected at the global extent. The Intergovernmental Panel on Climate Change (IPCC) used several general circulation models and scenarios of greenhouse gas emissions to project global climate trends. Projected changes by 2100 (IPCC 2007) include:

- An increase of 1 to 6 °C in the average global temperature.
  - Increases in temperature will differ by season. Increases in winter will be greater than increases in summer.
  - Changes in temperature will not be evenly distributed around the globe. Temperature will increase more in terrestrial areas than in oceans and more in high latitudes than in low latitudes. Increases in temperature are likely to exceed the global average in most of North America; all of Africa, Europe, and northern and central Asia; and most of Central and South America.

- An increase in global average annual precipitation, with changes varying from region to region.
  - Annual average precipitation will increase during winter over most of northern Europe, the Arctic, Canada, the northeastern United States, tropical and eastern Africa, the northern Pacific, Antarctica, northern Asia, and the Tibetan Plateau.
  - Annual average precipitation will decrease during winter in most of the Mediterranean, northern Africa, the northern Sahara, Central America, the Southwestern United States, the southern Andes, and southwestern Australia.
  - Summer precipitation will decrease over continental interiors owing to increases in evaporation.

- Extreme heat, heat waves, and heavy precipitation events will become more frequent.

If changes of the predicted magnitude occur, large portions of the Earth's surface may experience climates not found at present, and some current climates may disappear (Williams and others 2007). The new combinations of temperature and moisture regimes will likely result in disruption of existing host-pathogen combinations and formation of new combinations.

Western United States and Canada—

All regional climate models project that temperatures will increase in the Western United States by 2100. Most models project increases in winter temperature, decreases in moisture, and more frequent droughts throughout the region (Karl and others 2009, USDA FS 2003). Precipitation may increase slightly in winter, but the duration of seasonal heat and drought is likely to increase (Karl and others 2009, USDA FS 2003).

Regional projections for the Pacific Northwest (Mote and others 2003) suggest that temperature will increase from 0.5 to 2.5 °C by 2020, and from 1.5 to 3.2 °C by 2040. Precipitation across the region is projected to increase except during summer. In British Columbia, snowmelt may occur earlier and more rapidly, with a reduction in summer streamflows (Hamann and Wang 2006). Winters in northern British Columbia likely will be warmer and wetter. Across the region, winters likely will be wetter, and the proportion of precipitation falling as rain rather than snow is projected to increase (Pojar 2010, Spittlehouse 2008). In the southern half of the province, summers likely will be progressively warmer and drier. In the northern half of the province, summers initially may be cooler but ultimately are likely to be warmer and wetter.

Regional climate models all project that temperatures in California will increase substantially (Cayan and others 2006). Virtually all models project warming of at least a few degrees over the Sierra Nevada (Dettinger and others 2004). Projected increases in temperature by 2100 vary from 1.7 to 5.8 °C (Cayan and others 2006).

Models differ considerably in their projections of precipitation for California (Dettinger and others 2004). There is no evidence that the Mediterranean pattern of precipitation will change. All of the models examined (Cayan and others 2006) indicate that the vast majority of precipitation will continue to fall during winter storms from the North Pacific. Summer precipitation is projected to change little, and decreases in some of the models (Cayan and others 2006).

Most climate models project that the Southwestern United States will be warmer and drier. There will be fewer frost days; warmer temperatures in winter and spring, increased demand for water by plants, animals, and people; an increased frequency of extreme weather events; warmer nights; and declines in snowpack (Archer and Predick 2008a, 2008b; Weiss and Overpeck 2005).

Annual temperatures across the Colorado Plateau are projected to increase from 1.5 to 3.6 °C by 2050, and from 2.5 to 5.4 °C by 2100 (Garfin and others 2010). Summer temperatures are projected to increase more than winter temperatures (Ray and others 2008). Some models project an increase in annual mean precipitation, whereas others project a decrease of as much as 6 percent by 2100 (Garfin and others 2010, Ray and others 2008).

Projected changes in temperature and precipitation in different subregions of the intermountain West (Great Basin and Columbia Plateau) will vary as a function of storm patterns and differences in topography (Chambers and Pellant 2008). Temperatures in the region are projected to increase 2 to 5 °C by 2100. Projected changes in precipitation are inconsistent, with average changes near zero. Any increases are likely to occur largely in winter with little change or decreases in summer. Water availability will depend on the magnitude of increases in temperature and its effects on snowpack and evapotranspiration. Snowpacks have declined across the Western United States since about 1950, especially in the intermountain West. Evapotranspiration is projected to increase regardless of whether precipitation increases.

Effects on Tree Diseases

The literature on projected climate change and the potential effects on forest ecosystems and tree pathogens was recently summarized (Kliejunas and others 2009, Sturrock and others 2011). A synopsis is presented here.

The direction and magnitude of responses of tree diseases to climate change will differ. Changes will occur in the type, number, and relative importance of pathogens and diseases. Climate influences the survival and spread of pathogens as well as the susceptibility of their hosts. Climate change could alter stages and rates of development of the pathogen, modify host resistance, and lead to changes in the physiology of host–pathogen interactions. The most likely effects are changes in the geographical distribution of hosts and pathogens and changes in mortality of hosts, caused in part by changes in the efficacy of control strategies.

Although it is uncertain how specific forest pathogens will respond to climate change, some general inferences can be drawn:

The effects of climate change on individual plant diseases will depend on the ecosystem and climate conditions.

- The distribution of pathogens and diseases, and their influence on the status and trend of forests, will change. The ranges of some diseases will expand, whereas the ranges of other diseases will shift. The influence of pathogens on the status and function of forests may change coincident with changes in species composition and climate.
- Many pathogens currently are limited by winter temperature, and seasonal increases in temperature are expected to be greatest during winter. Therefore, both overwintering survival of pathogens and disease severity are likely to increase.

- Climate change will alter the epidemiology of plant diseases. Rapid climate change and unstable weather will make prediction of disease outbreaks more difficult.
- The rate at which pathogens evolve and overcome host resistance may increase.
- Because climate affects both host susceptibility to pathogens and pathogen reproduction and infection, the most substantial effect of climate change on plant diseases may be changes in interactions between biotic diseases and abiotic stressors.
- Climate change may facilitate invasion by new nonnative pathogens and thus new epidemics.

Diseases Posing Risk of Increased Damage

Disease reflects the interaction of a susceptible host, a virulent pathogen, and conducive environmental conditions. Susceptibility and virulence are affected by environmental conditions, and an increase in either or both will result in increased incidence of disease

Only a few observational or experimental studies or modeling efforts have documented pathogen responses to climate change. Responses will differ among pathogens and locations (Runion 2003, Sturrock 2007). Following are the descriptions of eight forest diseases that pose risks to forest ecosystems.

Dothistroma Needle Blight

Causal agents—

Dothistroma septosporum (Dorog.) Morelet (teleomorph=*Mycosphaerella pini* Rostr. [*Scirrhia pini* A. Funk & A.K. Parker]); *Dothistroma pini* Hulbary (teleomorph unknown); Dothidiales, Dothidiaceae.

Hosts—

D. septosporum: over 80 species of *Pinus, Pseudotsuga menziesii* (Mirb.) Franco, *Larix decidua* Mill., 5 species of *Picea; D. pini: Pinus nigra* Arnold.

Distribution—

D. septosporum: worldwide; *D. pini*: north-central United States, Ukraine.

History and Current Status

Dothistroma needle blight (figs. 1, 2, and 3), also referred to as red band needle blight because of the symptoms it causes on pine, is a conifer disease with a worldwide distribution (Bradshaw 2004, Gibson 1974) that causes substantial economic losses. Although first reported in Russia in 1911 (Doroguine 1911, Gibson 1974) and in the United States and elsewhere in Europe before 1920 (Brown and Webber 2008), it was not considered a serious disease until the 1950s (Bradshaw and others 2000). Most pines susceptible to infection are in stands less than 10 years old within plantations outside the natural range of the species. For example, the disease is

Figure 1—Lodgepole pine killed by *Dothistroma* near Kispiox, British Columbia.

absent from natural stands of radiata pine (*Pinus radiata* D. Don) in California but is present in stands planted north along the Pacific Coast, and in radiata pine plantations worldwide (Gibson 1972).

Dothistroma needle blight is primarily caused by *D. septosporum*. The teleomorph (sexual) state of the pathogen, *Mycosphaerella pini* (formerly *Scirrhia pini*), rarely has been observed. Recently, *D. pini* was found to cause Dothistroma needle blight in the north-central United States (Barnes and others 2004) and the Ukraine (Groenewald and others 2007). To date, no teleomorph of *D. pini* has been identified.

David Weaver, British Columbia Forest Service

Figure 2—Signs and symptoms of *Dothistroma* infection on needles of lodgepole pine.

Economic and Environmental Impacts

Damage is typically limited to reduced tree vigor and growth in response to defoliation (Bingham and others 1971, Patton 1997). Below about 40-percent crown infection, growth loss is proportional to the level of crown infection (Ades and others 1992, Bulman 1993, Van der Pas 1981). When crown infection exceeds 40 percent, the incremental loss is more than 40 percent, and there is virtually no growth if crown infection exceeds 80 percent (Gadgil 1974). Mortality is rare but has occurred in stands with successive years of severe defoliation (Bradshaw 2004).

Dothistroma needle blight has been a major constraint to the development of radiata pine plantations in New Zealand and Australia, Chile and other South American countries, and several African countries (Gibson 1972, 1974; Ivory 1967). Crop failure has been extensive in New Zealand's 400 000 ha of radiata pine (Marks and others 1989). Although mortality in New Zealand is rare, reduction in tree diameter and volume growth has caused losses on the order of $24 million per year (Bulman and others 2008). In Africa, the disease markedly reduced productivity of *P. radiata* plantations (Gibson and others 1964). In the United States, the disease has ruined ornamental and shelterbelt trees and plantations intended as sources of Christmas trees (Peterson 1966).

In northwest British Columbia, outbreaks of the disease have occurred periodically on lodgepole pine (*P. contorta* Douglas ex Louden var. *latifolia* Engelm. ex S. Watson) on some sites since the 1830s, with an increase in outbreak incidence and extent since the 1940s (Welsh and others 2009). In recent years, the impact of *D. septosporum* in British Columbia has increased dramatically (Woods 2003). An epidemic of *D. septosporum* was first detected in 1997 (Woods and others 2005). A survey of 41 000 ha in three forest districts from 2002 to 2004 detected the disease across 38 000 ha, with mortality occurring on 2700 ha. Even mature lodgepole pine trees were severely affected and dying (Worrall 2010). Lodgepole pine plantations between 15 and 20 years old had the most severe symptoms. Natural, mature stands of lodgepole pine also had substantial mortality (Woods 2003).

Dothistroma needle blight historically was rare in Great Britain, but dramatic increases in disease levels were noted from the late 1990s onward on Corsican pine (*Pinus nigra* ssp. *laricio* Maire) and occasionally on lodgepole pine (Archibald and Brown 2007, Brown and others 2003, Brown and Webber 2008). A 5-year moratorium on planting Corsican pine on public forests was implemented in 2007 (Brown and Webber 2008). The distribution and severity of the disease in France also increased in the late 1980s and early 1990s (Villebonne and Maugard 1999).

Figure 3—Mature lodgepole pine stand in central British Columbia affected by Dothistroma needle blight.

Disease Cycle

The disease cycle for both *Dothistroma* species is similar. Shortly after the death of needle tissue, the pathogen produces black fruiting bodies (stromata) that emerge through the dead epidermis. Conidial masses borne on the stromata typically begin to mature during the spring. Conidial production is largely dependent on sufficiently high temperature and duration of leaf wetness. Under optimal conditions, spores are released for up to 7 months (Karadzic 1989). Conidia may be released and cause infections at any point during the growing season when precipitation is falling (Peterson 1982) and temperatures are above 5 °C. Conidia are dispersed short distances by rain splash, and longer distances by wind-dispersed moisture droplets, mist, and low clouds (EPPO and CABI 1997). Ten hours or more of needle wetness is usually required for infection by *D. septosporum* (Bulman 1993, Gadgil 1974). The sexual state of the pathogen is formed in a similar way, but consists of linear black ascomata that contain ascospores (Gibson 1972).

Infection occurs on current-year or 1-year-old needles. Infection depends on several factors including the period of needle wetness, temperature, and the quantity of spores available for infection (Bulman 1993). Temperatures at which conidial germination and hyphal growth occur vary from a lower optimum of 15 °C (Gibson and others 1964) to an upper temperature threshold of 25 to 26 °C (Gibson and others 1964, Ivory 1972). Moisture is required for germination. The optimum temperature for successful establishment following germination is 12 to 18 °C when humidity is high (Brown and Webber 2008). Spores germinate and penetrate the needle through the stomata within 2 to 3 days (Bulman 2008).

Germinating spores produce a germ tube on which an appressorium (a swollen structure that adheres to the leaf surface and facilitates penetration) forms (Peterson and Walla 1978). From the appressorium, hyphae branch into intracellular and intercellular regions of the mesophyll layer of the needle tissue (Ivory 1972). In some hosts, distinct red bands (1 to 3 mm wide) appear around the needles within weeks of infection (Shain and Franich 1981). After 32 to 114 days, the host cells collapse and needle symptoms appear (Bradshaw 2004). The stromata generally mature and produce conidia a year or two after infection; in California and Oregon, the cycle may be completed in 1 year (Peterson 1982).

Environmental Drivers of Disease

Two factors seem to have contributed to the current *D. septosporum* epidemic in northwest British Columbia. First, although lodgepole pine is native, the species has been planted extensively since the early 1980s, increasing host abundance. Second, summer precipitation increased in the late 1990s. Woods and others (2005) found a strong positive relationship between the frequency of warm rain events and disease severity.

In Great Britain, springs are becoming earlier and warmer. Spring and summer precipitation has increased since the late 1990s compared with the previous 30 years (Brown and Webber 2008). Severe disease episodes appear to be associated with higher than average rainfall at the time of infection (Archibald and Brown 2007).

Although the teleomorph of *D. septosporum* has not been reported in Great Britain, Groenewald and others (2007) found both mating types in collections from the region. The increased frequency of the disease in Great Britain may also reflect increased genotypic diversity and associated adaptation if the two mating types of *D. septosporum* are widespread and are reproducing sexually (Brown and Webber 2008, Groenewald and others 2007). Also, the sexually produced ascospores are reported to be wind dispersed and therefore can move long distances (Gibson 1972).

Assessment and Analysis

Likelihood of increased disease damage[1]—

Warmer, drier—Low (moderately certain) (Applicable criteria: c, d).
Warmer, wetter—Moderate (very certain) (Applicable criteria: a, c, d).

Fungi that cause foliar disease may be more responsive to climate change than most other organisms that cause forest disease because their ability to sporulate and infect is strongly associated with changes in temperature and precipitation (Gadgil 1977, Hoff 1985, Peterson 1973).

The low level of disease detected in many regions with apparently suitable climate for the disease may reflect absence of hosts (Watt and others 2009). If the ranges of its hosts expand, the range of *Dothistroma* spp. could extend into Southeast China, Vietnam, Ireland, Western Australia, Venezuela, Guyana, Suriname, Panama, Turkey, Albania, and many countries bordering the Mediterranean Sea (Watt and others 2009).

Using slight variations of the CLIMEX (a model used to predict the effects of climate on species) parameter estimates used by Watt and others (2009), Venette[2] found that climatic conditions that support *Dothistroma* are likely to persist in the Western United States through 2080, even if *Dothistroma* is assumed to be heat-sensitive. The extent of climate conditions that support the pathogen may decrease by 2100 in eastern North America.[3] The favorable effect of warming on Dothistroma blight may lessen if decreased summer rainfall accompanies the warming.

Consequences of increased disease damage—

Moderate (moderately certain) (Applicable criteria: a, c).

Hosts in plantations, such as radiata pine in the Southern Hemisphere and lodgepole pine in British Columbia, have substantial commercial value. The pathogen typically reduces growth, and also may cause mortality of lodgepole pine in British Columbia, decreasing the economic value of the trees. The environmental effects of the disease currently are minimal, but collateral effects could increase if chemicals are used more extensively to control the disease.

---

[1] See pages 3 and 4 for definitions of the criteria used in the Assessment and Analysis section of each disease described.

[2] Venette, R.C. 2010. Climate modeling for a risk assessment for climate change and forest pathogens in western North America. Unpublished progress report. On file with: USDA Forest Service, Pacific Southwest Research Station, Albany, CA 94710.

[3] Venette, R.C. 2011. Personal communication. Research biologist, USDA Forest Service, Northern Research Station, 1561 Lindig Street, St. Paul, MN 55108.

Risk potential—

Warmer, drier—Low (2) (Likelihood of increased disease damage = low; consequences of increased disease damage = moderate).

Warmer, wetter—Moderate (4) (Likelihood of increased disease damage = moderate; consequences of increased disease damage = moderate).

Increases in precipitation may be more important than increases in temperature for increasing the spread and impact of the disease. As demonstrated in portions of British Columbia, if wetter than normal conditions prevail and inoculum potential increases, the potential for significant host mortality, rather than only growth reduction, exists.

Swiss Needle Cast

Causal agent—

Phaeocryptopus gaeumannii (Rohde) Petrak; Pleosporales, Venturiaceae.

Hosts—

Douglas-fir.

Distribution—

Native range of Douglas-fir and most areas where Douglas-fir has been introduced, including much of North America, Europe, and New Zealand.

History and Current Status

Phaeocryptopus gaeumannii (fig. 4) is native to the Pacific Northwest. For decades, Swiss needle cast was not considered to reduce forest health. Boyce (1940) reported that *P. gaeumannii* was widespread in western North America, but was inconspicuous or scarce on native Douglas-fir. However, he recognized that the pathogen produced abundant fruiting bodies on 1- and 2-year-old needles of diseased trees in Europe and caused extensive defoliation. Accumulating evidence supports Boyce's (1940) hypothesis that warm, humid summers with episodic rain are highly conducive to fungal growth and may allow the disease to reach epidemic levels, even in areas where it is native.

Since the early 1990s, a severe, unprecedented epidemic of Swiss needle cast has affected the coastal fog belt zone of Oregon, where Douglas-fir was not a dominant species in presettlement forests (Hansen and others 2000). Symptoms including chlorosis, premature needle loss, growth reduction, and abundant fruiting of the pathogen on 1- and 2-year-old needles are evident from Coquille and Bandon on the southern Oregon coast to Shelton, Washington, on Puget Sound; damage is concentrated in plantations near Tillamook, Oregon (Hansen and others 2000). Douglas-fir plantations that are 10 to 30 years old, in which microclimate generally is moist, are most visibly affected, but the fungus is present on seedlings after their first growing season in the field, as well as in mature stands. Severely diseased plantations are usually

Figure 4—Thin crown in a Douglas-fir infected with *Phaeocryptopus gaeumannii* along the Oregon Coast.

located at lower elevations west of the Coast Ranges. They are often in areas with summer fog and on sites previously occupied by species of spruce and hemlock or by hardwoods.

Economic and Environmental Impacts

The pathogen occurs over about 500 000 ha of Douglas-fir in Oregon. Approximately 160 000 ha are severely affected with Swiss needle cast, and some landowners in these areas are converting their Douglas-fir plantations to spruce and hemlock (Hansen and others 2002).

The primary mechanism of damage appears to be the fruiting bodies produced in the stomatal apertures. The fruiting bodies occlude the stomates and reduce rates of carbon dioxide assimilation (Manter and others 2000).

Mean and maximum decreases in basal area growth in Oregon are 20 percent and 55 percent, respectively (Maguire and others 2002, Mainwaring and others 2005). Douglas-fir radial growth was reduced by 85 percent at a severely diseased site (Black and others 2010). Vertical growth can decrease by about 25 percent. Decreases in growth can reduce the ability of planted Douglas-fir to compete with naturally seeded tree species (Maguire and others 2002). Decreases in growth have caused estimated losses of $200 million per year. Wood density and proportion of latewood to earlywood were higher in stands heavily infested (needle retention less than 2 years) with Swiss needle cast than in healthier stands (Johnson and others 2005).

Disease Cycle

Black fruiting bodies (pseudothecia) are produced in early winter in lines on the lower surface of infected needles. The pseudothecia are often produced on green needles that are 1 year or older. Ascospore release usually occurs from March through June, but can continue into August. The airborne ascospores typically infect current-year needles. When adequate moisture is present, the spores germinate and the fungus penetrates the needle. These infections are often latent for several years, but when the disease is severe, symptoms and fungal fruiting may occur as early as the year after needle production. The fungus grows throughout the needle. Fruiting bodies form in the stomata in autumn and winter and mature the following spring. The proportion of infected needles may become substantial before defoliation occurs (Smith 1978).

Environmental Drivers of Disease

Increased severity of Swiss needle cast in the Oregon Coast Range reflects introduction of Douglas-fir, increases in winter temperatures, and increases in precipitation in the winter and spring (Stone and others 2008). Occurrence of the disease in the Pacific Northwest is positively correlated with degree-day accumulation during winter and leaf wetness hours from spring through autumn (warm winters and wet summers) (Manter and others 2005). Since 1970, winter temperatures increased by 0.2 to 0.4 °C and spring precipitation by 0.7 to 1.5 cm per decade (Stone and others 2008).

In southern British Columbia, Hood (1982) observed a positive correlation between precipitation, particularly spring rainfall, and relative abundance of *P. gaeumannii*. In New Zealand, winter mean temperature explained approximately 80 percent of the variation in severity of disease caused by *P. gaeumannii* (Stone and others 2007). Reductions in needle retention owing to *P. gaeumannii* infection were positively related to a projected increase in air temperature of 0.144 °C from 2006 to 2090 (Watt and others 2010).

Assessment and Analysis

Likelihood of increased disease damage—
Warmer, drier—Low (reasonably certain) (Applicable criterion: c).
Warmer, wetter—Moderate (very certain) (Applicable criteria: a, c).

An increase of Swiss needle cast in the Oregon Coast Range is associated with long-term warming trends during the late winter and early spring (Black and others 2010). Winter temperature in the Pacific Northwest is projected to continue increasing by approximately 0.4 °C per decade through 2050 (Stone and others 2008). A decrease in precipitation would likely decrease the probability of damage to Douglas-fir from *P. gaeumannii*.

Consequences of increased disease damage—
Moderate (reasonably uncertain) (Applicable criteria: a, c).

Douglas-fir has commercial value, but the pathogen attacks only that host and only causes significant damage in a limited area of the host's range. The disease does not typically cause mortality or other direct environmental effects.

Risk potential—
Warmer, drier—Low (2) (Likelihood of increased disease damage = low; consequences of increased disease damage = moderate).

Warmer, wetter—Moderate (4) (Likelihood of increased disease damage = moderate; consequences of increased disease damage = moderate).

Predicted warmer temperatures, along with sufficient moisture, will favor the pathogen and increase disease incidence on Douglas-fir.

Sudden Oak Death; Ramorum Blight

Pathogen—

Phytophthora ramorum Werres, de Cock & Man in't Veld;
Peronosporales, Pythiaceae.

Hosts—

More than 130 species of hardwoods, conifers, shrubs, herbaceous plants, and
ferns in over 75 genera and at least 37 families.

Distribution—

United States: in native woodlands in Curry County, Oregon, and 14 coastal
counties (Alameda, Contra Costa, Humboldt, Lake, Marin, Mendocino, Monterey,
Napa, San Francisco, San Mateo, Santa Clara, Santa Cruz, Solano, and Sonoma)
in California; detected and eradicated in nurseries (and residential plantings of
infected nursery stock) in several states.

Canada: Nurseries in British Columbia and some related residential plantings
(eradication efforts underway).

Europe: Detected and under official control in nurseries or gardens in Belgium,
Czech Republic, Denmark, Estonia, Finland, France, Germany, Ireland, Italy,
Latvia, Lithuania, Luxembourg, the Netherlands, Norway, Poland, Portugal,
Slovenia, Spain (including Mallorca), Sweden, Switzerland, and the entire United
Kingdom, including the Channel Islands; under eradication in forests in the United
Kingdom and the Netherlands.

History and Current Status

Phytophthora ramorum, the cause of sudden oak death (fig. 5) and ramorum
blight, was first detected in 1993 in Germany and the Netherlands on ornamental
rhododendrons (*Rhododendron* spp.) (Werres and others 2001). In June 2000, the
pathogen was isolated from dying tanoak (*Notholithocarpus densiflorus* (Hook. &
Arn.) Manos, C.H. Cannon & S. Oh) trees in California (Rizzo and others 2002).
In December 2000, *P. ramorum* was recovered from rhododendrons with leaf
symptoms in a Santa Cruz County, California, nursery surrounded by dying oaks
(Garbelotto and Rizzo 2005). The pathogen was detected in July 2001 in a forest
in Curry County, Oregon.

Following the first detection in a nursery in California in 2001, the pathogen
was found in 20 nurseries in Oregon, Washington, and British Columbia. Dispersal
of the pathogen in the nursery trade in North America and in Europe became
a major concern. In 2004, *P. ramorum* was detected in two large nurseries in

Figure 5—Sudden oak death of tanoak on Mount Tamalpais, Marin County, California.

southern California and in one nursery each in Oregon and Washington. It was subsequently determined that these nurseries had shipped potentially infected plants to over 1,200 nurseries in 39 states (Frankel 2008). *Phytophthora ramorum* continues to disperse via the nursery and ornamental trade in both North America and Europe.

Because *P. ramorum* was present in Germany and the Netherlands, surveillance for the pathogen began in England and Wales in July 2001 and subsequently in other European countries (Brasier and others 2006). In the United Kingdom, *P. ramorum* was first detected in a nursery in April 2002 on *Viburnum tinus* L. (Lane and others 2003). *Phytophthora ramorum* was subsequently found on southern red oak trees (*Quercus falcata* Michx.) in the United Kingdom, and on European beech (*Fagus sylvatica* L.) and American northern red oak (*Q. rubra* L.) in the Netherlands (Brasier and others 2004). As in the United States, the range of *P. ramorum* in Europe is extensive and increasing. The pathogen affects a large number of plant genera and species in the ornamental nursery trade and in parks, gardens, and woodlands. The pathogen now has an extensive distribution but low incidence in the European Union's nursery industry (Sansford and others 2009). *Phytophthora ramorum* is subject to official governmental control in the countries where it is known to occur (19 European Union member states plus Norway, Switzerland, the United States, and Canada).

The geographic origin of *P. ramorum* is unknown. Before the mid-1990s, the species had not been reported in the United States or Europe. The European and North American populations are distinct and were transported independently from another, unknown, location. Populations of *P. ramorum* are clonal, consisting of three lineages, NA1, NA2, and EU1 (Grünwald and others 2008a, Ivors and others 2006, Martin 2008).

Three different diseases are attributed to *P. ramorum* (Hansen and others 2002). The first, known as sudden oak death in the United States and ramorum bleeding canker in Europe, is characterized by bleeding bark cankers on the bole, which can be lethal. The second disease, ramorum shoot dieback, results from foliar infection or infection of stems. The third, ramorum leaf blight, results from foliar infection. Thus, the diverse symptoms produced by *P. ramorum* depend on the host plant and host part affected. Individual plant species can display more than one disease type (e.g., leaf blight, shoot dieback, and bleeding cankers on tanoak. A comparison of symptoms of sudden oak death and ramorum blight (a combination of shoot dieback and leaf blight) published by Grünwald and others (2008b) is presented here in modified form in table 2.

Table 2—Comparison of symptoms of sudden oak death and ramorum blight, both caused by *Phytophthora ramorum*

Disease	Symptoms	Host categories	Typical hosts	Geography/environment
Sudden oak death	Stem cankers; bleeding cankers	Forest and garden trees	Coast live oak, tanoak, European beech, others	North American forests, European gardens
Ramorum blight	Foliar and twig blight; tip and shoot dieback; leaf blight	Ornamental trees and woody shrubs; understory plants	California bay laurel, rhododendron, viburnum, pieris, coast redwood (*Sequoia sempervirens* (D. Don) Endl.), Japanese larch, tanoak, others	North American nurseries and forests, European nurseries, forest plantations and gardens

Source: Modified from Grünwald and others 2008b.

Economic and Environmental Impacts

Many *P. ramorum* hosts are grown for their commercial, ecological, or social value. Tanoak, coast live oak (*Q. agrifolia* Nee), and black oak (*Q. kelloggii* Newberry) in the United States die relatively quickly after the onset of symptoms. Economic impacts in urban areas include reduction in property value and costs for removal of dead trees that may injure people or increase the probability of fire. Current economic impacts to the nursery and ornamental industry in the United States are estimated to be in the range of $100 to $300 million. Canada spent about $8.5 million in one year on control. Current economic impacts in the European Union are estimated as minor to moderate (Sansford and others 2009).

The current impact on nursery-grown ornamental species is thought to be moderate within the areas in which *P. ramorum* occurs in the European Union, United States, and Canada. Quarantine restrictions imposed on the horticultural industry have had substantial economic consequences. The costs of phytosanitary controls are considerable (Sansford and others 2009), but not quantified.

In the United States, environmental impacts of *P. ramorum* have been greatest in coastal woodlands in California and southwestern Oregon. Mortality of tanoak and oaks are resulting in changes in forest composition, loss of habitat for animals, increases in soil erosion, and a substantial increase in fuel loads near heavily populated urban-woodland interfaces. In Europe, oak is a dominant native species in forest and savanna-woodland ecosystems. There are approximately 200 million oak trees in the United Kingdom. Their loss could have a major impact on soil erosion, hydrology, and sedimentation in rivers. Other possible effects include loss of associated plants and animals and a reduction in tourism, cultural values, and local woodland-based economies (Sansford and others 2009, Sansford and Woodhall 2007).

Disease Cycle

The life cycle of *P. ramorum* is similar to that of other aerial *Phytophthora* species. The pathogen produces sporangia on the surfaces of infected leaves and twigs of foliar hosts that can be splash-dispersed to neighboring hosts or transported longer distances by wind and rain (Davidson and others 2005). Moderate temperatures (18 to 21 °C) accompanied by rain or overhead irrigation facilitate the spread of and infection by spores. *Phytophthora ramorum* is also spread downstream of infested areas in rivers and streams, and can be carried in soil or infected plants. On contact with a host, the sporangia germinate directly, by emergence of hyphae through the sporangial wall, or indirectly, by producing zoospores that encyst, penetrate the host, and initiate a new infection. Chlamydospores are readily produced in infected plant material and serve as resting structures in soil, allowing the pathogen to survive adverse conditions (Shishkoff 2007, Tooley and others 2008). Moisture is essential for survival and sporulation, and the duration, frequency, and timing of winter rain events plays a key role in inoculum production.

In California forests, *P. ramorum* epidemics are driven by presence of California bay laurel (*Umbellularia californica* (Hook. & Arn.) Nutt., on which *P. ramorum* sporulates prolifically (Davidson and others 2005). In southwest Oregon, tanoak is the key foliar host and inoculum producer (Rizzo and others 2005). In Europe, heavily infected wild *Rhododendron ponticum* L. in the understory is responsible for producing inoculum that infects neighboring trees (Brasier and others 2004). The pathogen also sporulates heavily on planted Japanese larch (*Larix kaempferi* (Lamb.) Carr) in England, Ireland, and Scotland (Webber and others 2010).

Environmental Drivers of Disease

Temperatures for optimal growth of *P. ramorum* are between 18 and 22 °C (Werres and others 2001). Many species of *Phytophthora* germinate indirectly at temperatures below about 12 °C and directly at higher temperatures (Ribeiro 1983). Maximum levels of zoospore germination occur at 100 percent humidity or water potentials of 1. Depending on the water potential, germination can occur between temperatures of 10 to 30 °C (Kessel and others 2007, Turner and Jennings 2008). The prevalence of infection of California bay laurel leaves averaged 92 percent at 18 °C, but only 50 percent at 12 °C and 37 percent at 30 °C (Garbelotto and others 2003). A minimum of 6 to 12 consecutive hours of free water is a prerequisite for the infection of California bay laurel leaves (Garbelotto and others 2003). Infection by zoospores tends to occur on plant parts where water accumulates, such as leaf tips.

In California mixed-evergreen forests, sporulation and inoculum production is seasonal, largely dependent on rainfall events and temperature. Sporangial production in redwood/tanoak forests begins soon after the start of the rainy season (Maloney and others 2002). In California, *P. ramorum* is commonly recovered from rain traps from December into spring, peaking during warm rains in May (Davidson and others 2005). At one study site in a mixed-evergreen forest, detectable levels of *P. ramorum* inoculum were present primarily during the winter rainy season and were absent during the hot, dry summer (Davidson and others 2005). In contrast, *P. ramorum* inoculum (most likely dehiscent sporangia) in infested forests of southwest Oregon can be produced throughout the year whenever water is available (Hansen and others 2008).

Spore production differs yearly as well as seasonally. In California, relatively high levels of winter and spring rainfall extending into early summer are often followed by high levels of disease (Davidson and others 2005, Rizzo and others 2005). Epidemic mortality of coast live oak occurred 1 to 2 years after high spring rainfall in the El Niño years of 1998 and 2005 (Davidson and others 2005, Rizzo and others 2005). In Oregon, Kanaskie and others (2008) attributed an unexpected expansion of the disease from sites where eradication efforts were being conducted to 2 consecutive years with an unusually wet spring and early summer. Hansen and others (2008) reported that rain in late May following a dry April triggered an infection event at two sites, resulting in dieback, subsequent sprouting of tanoak, and numerous new *P. ramorum* bole infections.

Assessment and Analysis

Likelihood of increased disease damage—

Warmer, drier—Low (moderately certain) (Applicable criteria: c, d, e).

Warmer, wetter—High (very certain) (Applicable criteria a, c, d, e).

Increased precipitation during spring is likely to be associated with increased prevalence of the pathogen in areas where it already occurs and expansion of the pathogen to new locations. Chlamydospores and zoospores of the pathogen can survive more than 30 days under moist conditions in the laboratory, but less than 30 minutes when the relative humidity is less than 30 percent (Davidson and others 2002).

Magarey and others (2008) used the North Carolina State University—Animal and Plant Health Inspection Service Plant Pest Forecasting System (NAPPFAST) to project *P. ramorum* infection across the conterminous United States as a function of temperature and moisture. Venette and Cohen (2006) used the CLIMEX model to identify areas of the United States where *P. ramorum* might occur. Venette (2009) also used the CLIMEX model to quantify the potential change in distribution of habitat and in habitat quality for *P. ramorum* on the basis of climate scenarios. The model suggested that high-quality habitat in the contiguous United States currently extends along the west coast from approximately Monterey, California, to the vicinity of Puget Sound, Washington. Large areas of habitat also occur in the Eastern United States. On the basis of projections from the Canadian General Circulation Model-1 (CGCM1), Venette projected that the extent of high-quality habitat will decrease substantially in the Eastern United States, but will increase in Washington, Oregon, and California. By 2050, habitat will extend from Los Angeles, California, to the Puget Sound area in Washington. Inland expansion of habitat by 2080 is projected to be modest. In the Eastern United States, small, isolated patches of high-quality habitat are projected to occur in far western North Carolina, the northeast quarter of West Virginia and from northern New Jersey to southern Massachusetts. The shift in distribution seems to result from changes in biological heat stress.

Consequences of increased disease damage—

High (reasonably uncertain) (Applicable criteria: a, b, c, d, e).

Numerous hosts of *P. ramorum*, including forest trees and ornamental plants, have substantial economic value. The Animal and Plant Health Inspection Service risk assessment for *P. ramorum* (Cave and others 2008) rated the environmental impact of the pathogen as high on the basis of its potential to disrupt native ecosystems and vegetation types within its current geographic range, the need for additional control programs, and the potential of the pathogen to directly or indirectly reduce probability of persistence of species listed as threatened or endangered under the federal Endangered Species Act (ESA 1973). Reasonable uncertainty reflects the difficulty in estimating environmental costs associated with use of herbicides to prevent, eradicate, or suppress the pathogen; effects on protected species; and effects on ecological processes such as water and nutrient cycling (Cave and others 2008).

Risk potential—
Warmer, drier—Moderate (3) (Likelihood of increased disease damage = low; consequences of increased disease damage = high).

Warmer, wetter—Very high (9) (Likelihood of increased disease damage = high; consequences of increased disease damage = high).

Continued warming would increase areas suitable climatically for the pathogen, resulting in increased mortality if the pathogen is introduced to those areas. However, moisture must be sufficient for pathogen sporulation and infection.

White Pine Blister Rust

Pathogen—

Cronartium ribicola J.C. Fischer in Rabenhorst.

Hosts—

In North America, eastern white pine (*Pinus strobus* L.), western white pine (*P. monticola* Douglas ex D. Don), sugar pine (*P. lambertiana* Douglas), southwestern white pine (*P. strobiformis* Engelm.), whitebark pine (*P. albicaulis* Douglas), limber pine (*P. flexilis* James), foxtail pine (*P. balfouriana* Grev. & Balf.), and Rocky Mountain bristlecone pine (*P. aristata* Engelm.).

Distribution—

North America, Europe, Asia.

History and Current Status

Cronartium ribicola was introduced from Asia into North America in the early 1900s on seedlings of eastern white pine grown in Europe. The rust was introduced on numerous occasions into the Eastern United States, then on nursery stock into the Western United States (Bega 1978).

White pine blister rust (fig. 6) now occurs in the northeastern and Western United States and in the Great Lakes region. It was introduced into British Columbia in 1910 and has spread from there throughout most white pine regions of Washington, Oregon, California, Idaho, Montana, Wyoming, and Colorado (Bega 1978, Mielke 1943). All but one species of white pine (Great Basin bristlecone pine, *Pinus longaeva* D.K. Bailey) endemic to western Canada and the United States are currently infected.

Economic and Environmental Impacts

Blister rust infection of pines results in branch dieback, reproductive failure, and tree mortality. In North America, white pine blister rust has caused more damage and costs more to control than any other conifer disease (Bega 1978). The number of western white pine trees has decreased 90 percent in northern Idaho, where the species has been reduced to a minor component in stands it had historically dominated (Neuenschwander and others 1999). Since the 1920s, millions of dollars have been spent on the eradication of the alternate host, *Ribes* (currants and gooseberries). Thousands of white pine stands have been severely damaged. In the Western United States and Canada, mortality in some stands has been complete (Bega 1978). The size of populations of western white pine, sugar pine, whitebark pine, and several other species have declined substantially (Zeglan and others 2010).

Figure 6—White pine blister rust on southwestern white pine in the Sacramento Mountains, New Mexico.

The pathogen interacts with other stressors to induce mortality. The synergistic effects of *C. ribicola*, drought, increasing temperatures, and mountain pine beetle (*Dendroctonus ponderosae*) are considered the ultimate cause of the high mortality observed in many high-elevation populations of white pine (Gibson and others 2008, Kegley and others 2004, Logan and Powell 2001, Tomback and Achuff 2010).

Disease Cycle

Cronartium ribicola is a heteroecious (requires at least two hosts to complete its life cycle), macrocyclic rust that produces five distinct spore stages during its life cycle. The pathogen alternates between five-needle pines and *Ribes* spp. (occasionally *Pedicularis* spp. and *Castilleja* spp.; McDonald and others 2006). Thin-walled basidiospores, produced on *Ribes* leaves, are wind-borne up to a few kilometers and infect through stomates of pine needles in autumn. The pathogen grows into and down the branch toward the main stem. It grows in the phloem and bark with no visible symptoms for at least 3 years before spores are produced. Spermatia are formed in the spring of the third or fourth year, followed a year later by the production of aeciospores in white blisters that break through the bark. Thick-walled aeciospores are wind-dispersed over distances up to about 480 km and are capable of infecting the telial host (*Ribes* spp.; occasionally *Pedicularis* and *Castilleja*).

Approximately 10 days after infection of leaves, urediospores develop and are produced on the leaves throughout the summer. Urediospores are able to reinfect *Ribes* spp., thus intensifying the disease. In autumn, teliospores and basidiospores are produced on *Ribes* spp., and the basidiospores transmit the disease back to pines to complete the life cycle.

Environmental Drivers of Disease

The environmental requirements for blister rust infection are well-documented (Bega 1960, Mielke 1943, Spaulding 1922, Van Arsdel 1954). Van Arsdel and others (2006) summarized the literature and their observations on the environmental conditions for growth, sporulation, germination, and infection. Although weather requirements for infection are complex, the disease apparently has no environmental limits wherever white pines and *Ribes* spp. cohabit (Kinloch 2003). Climate currently is not a limiting factor in white pine blister rust distribution in British Columbia (Campbell and Antos 2000). The pathosystem commonly displays a wave year phenomenon when especially favorable weather facilitates substantial increases in rust spread and intensification (Kinloch 2003, Peterson 1971).

Blister rust is considered a cool weather disease. In Wisconsin, rust distribution and average July temperatures were negatively correlated. Rust infection was more extensive where July temperatures averaged less than 21 °C. Where the average was higher, rust was usually confined to cool, moist microclimates (Van Arsdel and others 1961).

Inoculum production—
Aeciospores are usually produced in the spring at temperatures from 16 to 28 °C. They are released when the air is saturated (Van Arsdel and others 2006). The optimum temperature range for urediospore production is from 14 to 20 °C, with a night minimum of 2 °C (Van Arsdel and others 2006).

Telia seldom develop well when temperatures are high (Riker and others 1947). In the sugar pine region of California and Oregon, rains from large-scale cyclonic warm fronts increase soil moisture and relative humidity near ground level. Teliospore production on *Ribes* begins a minimum of 2 weeks after aecial or uredial infection. The favorable range for teliospore formation is 1 to 20 °C, with an optimum at 16 °C. Temperatures greater than 20 °C or 0° for 12 hours at formation affect germination, but teliospores can recover from freezing (Van Arsdel and others 2006). Production is stimulated by cool temperatures, and inhibited by 3 consecutive days above 28 °C, night minima above 20 °C, or daily maxima above 35 °C (Van Arsdel and others 1956).

Basidiospore production begins when viable teliospores are present and moisture is present as free water or relative humidity exceeds 97 percent. Germination is most successful at 100 percent relative humidity when teliospores are in contact with water (Van Arsdel and others 2006).

Inoculum dispersal—
Not only moisture and air temperature but air circulation affect the timing and pattern of rust spread (Van Arsdel 1965). Calm and clear nights cause radiant heat loss and down-slope flow of water-saturated air that controls patterns of local teliospore germination, basidiospore transport, and pine infection (Kimmey and Wagener 1961).

Establishment of infection—
Spore germination and infection of pine needles requires 48 hours with 100 percent relative humidity and temperatures not exceeding 20 °C.

The minimum time for *Ribes* infection by aeciospores is 7 to 8 days of temperatures of 5 to 24 °C for production, followed by 12 hours of saturated air for spore release, an additional 5 hours at 16 to 20 °C and greater than 97 percent relative humidity, and the presence of wet *Ribes* leaves for germination and penetration (Van Arsdel and others 2006). High foliar nitrogen concentrations increase susceptibility in pines and *Ribes* (McDonald and Dekker-Robertson 1998, Van Arsdel 1972), so association with nitrogen-fixing plants or artificial fertilization may increase *Ribes* susceptibility.

Survival—
Cronartium ribicola needs living host tissue to survive. Fires that remove soil organic layers kill *Ribes* in the seedbank, but fires of low to moderate intensity allow *Ribes* to regenerate (Arno 2000) from seed in lower levels of the soil profile and from living bases of surviving plants (Littlefield 1930, Miller 2000, Moss and Wellner 1953). Fire stimulates surviving seed to germinate (Lyon and Stickney 1976). Seedling establishment is greatest in the first year after fire (Quick 1954). *Ribes* establishment can be particularly high where slash piles have been burned (Moss and Wellner 1953).

Assessment and Analysis

Likelihood of increased disease damage—

Warmer, drier—Low (reasonably certain) (Applicable criteria: c, e).

Warmer, wetter—Low (moderately certain) (Applicable criteria: c, e).

Although increases in precipitation likely increase habitat quality for the pathogen, projected increases in temperature do not. Projected changes in climate to 2100 would affect not only the rust disease but the distribution and status of white pine populations. The extent of habitat for whitebark pine (Warwell and others 2007) is likely to decrease substantially, with the species shifting to relatively cool locations at higher elevations and latitudes.

Some climate scenarios project decreases in summer precipitation in the Rocky Mountains but increases in the Southwestern United States (Bartlein and others 1997, Kliejunas and others 2009). The probability of wave year occurrence of the disease decreases as temperatures increase and precipitation decreases (Kinloch 2003), possibly resulting in less rust infection. The incidence of the disease may decrease in areas such as the southern Sierra Nevada if temperatures increase and precipitation decreases. Early season infection of pine is common in the coastal regions of British Columbia (Hunt 2005). In the southern Sierra Nevada, infection of white pine normally coincides with spring rains and summer thunderstorms (Kinloch and Dulitz 1990). A long and cool winter is required before *Ribes* break dormancy and become susceptible, telial hosts (Zambino 2010).

Consequences of increased disease damage—

High (reasonably certain) (Applicable criteria: a, b, c, d, e).

In general, an increase in incidence and severity of blister rust would increase economic loss of timber from western white pine and sugar pine, and have a substantial adverse effect on high-elevation white pines, some of which are narrowly distributed.

Risk potential—

Warmer, drier—Moderate (3) (Likelihood of increased disease damage = low; consequences of increased disease damage = high).

Warmer, wetter—Moderate (3) (Likelihood of increased disease damage = low; consequences of increased disease damage = high).

A warmer climate, along with drier environmental conditions, would reduce rust sporulation and infection. Although wetter conditions would favor the pathogen, warmer temperatures would not.

Cytospora Canker of Alder

Causal agent—

Valsa melanodiscus G.H. Otth [anamorph = *Cytospora umbrina* (Bonord) Sacc.]; Diaporthales, Valsaceae.

Hosts—

Thinleaf alder (*Alnus incana* (L.) Moench ssp. *tenuifolia* (Nutt.) Breitung), Sitka alder (*A. viridis* (Chaix) DC. ssp. *sinuata* (Regel) A. Löve & D. Löve), green alder (*A. viridis* (Chaix) DC).

Distribution—

Alaska, British Columbia, northern New Mexico, Colorado, southern Wyoming.

History and Current Status

Cytospora spp. (anamorphs of *Valsa* spp.) are stem and branch canker pathogens of trees. The genus is distributed worldwide, infecting more than 70 species (Kepley and Jacobi 2000). Members of the genus are typically facultative parasites—usually saprobes, but capable of infecting trees and causing cankers when the hosts are stressed.

An alder canker disease associated with the fungal pathogen *Valsa melanodiscus* (anamorph = *Cytospora umbrina*) (Stanoz and others 2008) has caused damage to alders since the late 1980s in Colorado and nearby areas, and since about 2002 in Alaska (Trummer 2006, Worrall 2009). The pathogen kills vascular tissues; causes elongated, girdling stem cankers; and frequently causes stem dieback and mortality. Dieback and mortality of thinleaf alder within riparian areas is occurring in Colorado and adjacent areas and in south-central and interior Alaska. Sitka alder, and to a lesser degree green alder, are also affected in Alaska (USDA FS 2007). The pathogen is native and was first reported in Alaska in the 1930s (Trummer 2006).

Economic and Environmental Impacts

Cytospora canker of thinleaf alder (fig. 7) is currently epidemic in the southern Rocky Mountains, Alaska, and other areas of western North America (Trummer 2006, Worrall 2009). Of standing stems surveyed in Colorado and adjoining areas, 37 percent were dead and 29 percent were diseased (Worrall 2009). Similar damage has been reported across thousands of acres in south-central and interior Alaska (Trummer 2006).

In Alaska, alder is a keystone early successional tree, and mortality may have adverse long-term ecological consequences (Rohrs-Richey 2008). In the Rocky Mountain region, thinleaf alder is often a dominant plant in high-elevation riparian

Figure 7—Orange-red spore tendrils of *Cytospora umbrina* on thinleaf alder in the southern Rocky Mountains.

areas. The alder stabilize soils, fix nitrogen, provide shelter for terrestrial animals, and shade streams, which improves fish habitat quality (Worrall 2009).

Disease Cycle

Conidia, produced in conidiomata in the spring and throughout the growing season, are transmitted by splashing or windblown rain. Infection sites include injured or dead host bark tissue; spores typically are unable to invade healthy bark. The spores germinate under moist conditions and penetrate the bark. Once established in the bark tissue, the fungus kills bark cells, girdles the branch or tree, and produces asexual or sexual fruiting structures. *Cytospora* fungi produce spores in tiny, black, pimple-like fruiting bodies, which break out through the bark. Ascomata (fruiting bodies of the sexual state) typically form in the summer and autumn.

Environmental Drivers of Disease

Temperature-induced drought stress may increase host susceptibility and disease severity. In Colorado and adjacent areas, rapid canker growth and killing of branches and stems occurred from late June to late July, when temperatures were at the annual maximum and humidity was low (Worrall and others 2010). Canker growth ceased with the arrival of monsoonal precipitation despite the persistence of high maximum temperatures for several weeks. The increase in atmospheric moisture likely reduced transpiration and associated moisture stress. Projected increases in temperature will likely cause the *Cytospora* canker epidemic to continue and become more severe (Worrall and others 2010).

Assessment and Analysis

Likelihood of increased disease damage—
Warmer, drier—High (moderately certain) (Applicable criteria: a, b, c, e).
Warmer, wetter—Moderate (reasonably uncertain) (Applicable criteria: a, c, e).

Warmer temperatures and drier conditions will stress the host, increasing its susceptibility to infection and to canker growth. Wetter conditions may reduce the host moisture stress, slowing or stopping canker growth.

Consequences of increased disease damage—
Moderate (reasonably certain) (Applicable rating criteria: b, d).

Infection often results in host mortality. Although alder has limited economic value, it is a keystone species in riparian areas, and its loss from those areas would have substantial environmental consequences.

Risk potential—
Warmer, drier—High (6) (Likelihood of increased disease damage = high; consequences of increased pest damage = moderate).

Warmer, wetter—Moderate (4) (Likelihood of increased disease damage = moderate; consequences of increased disease damage = moderate).

Dwarf Mistletoes

Causal agent—

Arceuthobium spp.; Santalales, Viscaceae.

Hosts—

The six genera of the Pinaceae (*Abies, Larix, Picea, Pinus, Pseudotsuga,* and *Tsuga*), Cupressaceae.

Distribution—

North America, Asia, Europe, parts of northern Africa.

History and Current Status

Dwarf mistletoes (fig. 8) are parasitic flowering plants that infect conifers, producing characteristic aerial shoots that are leafless and yellow to orange or green to brown. *Arceuthobium* is defined by its bicolored, explosively dehiscent fruits. Many of the species are specific to individual commercially important conifer species in western North America (western Canada, Western United States, and Mexico) (Geils and others 2002).

The distribution of a dwarf mistletoe species is generally centered within the range of its principal host or hosts (Hawksworth and Weins 1996). Management

Figure 8—A dead mature western hemlock tree with hemlock dwarf mistletoe infections created a canopy gap in a coastal Alaska forest.

history explains the greatest proportion of variance in abundance of dwarf mistletoe in stands. Climate and topography also influence the current distribution of dwarf mistletoe (Hawksworth and Weins 1996).

Economic and Environmental Impacts

In the Western United States, *Arceuthobium* species cause an estimated loss of 11.3×10^6 m^3 (3×10^9 board feet) per year via mortality and reduction in growth (Drummond 1982, Hawksworth and Wiens 1996). Annual mortality and growth loss caused by dwarf mistletoe ranges from 10 percent of the commercial harvest in the northern Rockies (Loomis and others 1985) to 50 percent in Arizona and New Mexico (Reich and others 1991). Infection results in reductions in tree growth, seed and cone production, and wood quality, and in increased tree mortality and host susceptibility to attacks from pathogens and insects (Giles and Hawksworth 2002, Hawksworth and Wiens 1970). In addition, *Arceuthobium* infection often results in formation of dense masses of branches (brooms) on the host that create fuel ladders into tree crowns (Hawksworth and Wiens 1970).

Disease Cycle

Arceuthobium species are disseminated primarily by explosive seed. The berries ripen in the late summer or autumn and burst, shooting their sticky seeds as much as 15 m horizontally. The seeds adhere to needles, twigs, branches, and trunks and germinate the following spring. Host infection occurs when the rootlike structure (haustorium) from a germinated seed penetrates the bark. The haustorial system grows within the wood and provides the parasite with water and nutrients supplied by the host tree. The dwarf mistletoe plant continues to grow and spread in the host. Shoots of the obligate parasite form within 2 to 4 years, and fruits are produced in another 1 to 2 years (Scharpf 1978).

Environmental Drivers of Disease

Although dwarf mistletoes do not require specific environmental conditions after infection, environmental factors that stress the host affect the potential impact of the dwarf mistletoe. Dwarf mistletoes play a substantial role in mortality of trees that are stressed by drought or other factors. For example, the interactive effects of *Arceuthobium* and bark beetles are responsible for 40 to 60 percent of the pine mortality in southern California during years of average precipitation. Mortality is more frequent in the presence of other stress factors, such as drought, air pollution, or extremely high stand density (Schultz and Allison 1982, Schultz and Kliejunas 1982). Wood and others (1979) attributed 90 percent of the mortality of Jeffrey pines (*Pinus jeffreyi* Balf.) at Laguna Mountain in southern California to the synergistic effects of California flatheaded borer (*Melanophila californica*), western dwarf mistletoe (*A. campylopodum*), and annosus root disease, caused by *Heterobadision annosum*. In the central Sierra Nevada, susceptibility of red fir (*Abies magnifica* A. Murray) to infection by fir engraver (*Scolytus ventralis*) increases in response to severe drought, high tree density, annosus root disease, and dwarf mistletoe (Frankel and others 1988). Childs (1960) reported that death of conifer branches in the Pacific Northwest following an unusually hot summer in 1958 and an unusually dry summer in 1959 was extensive in trees stressed by dwarf mistletoe and other agents. Childs (1960) also suggested that the death of branches infected by dwarf mistletoe may reduce inoculum and thus reduce dwarf mistletoe spread.

Surveys during the 1976–1977 drought in California estimated that 12.3 million trees (equivalent to about 30 000 m³ of wood) in diverse locations and forest types had died. Forest insects and pathogens explained 98 percent of the lost volume. Of this loss, 65 percent was attributed to a combination of dwarf mistletoe and root diseases that increased the susceptibility of the hosts to drought stress (Byler 1978, Craig 1979). Later surveys in California also indicated that trees infected with dwarf mistletoe were the first to die during drought (Byler 1978). Dwarf mistletoe increased the susceptibility of many stands to invasion by insects and have induced 60 to 80 percent of all Jeffrey pine mortality in years of severe drought (Jenkinson 1990). The occurrence and severity of effects of dwarf mistletoe on ponderosa pine in southwest Colorado were greatest in dry habitats (Merrill and others 1987). Wilson and Tkacz (1992) reported that severe drought, dense stands, and presence of pinyon dwarf mistletoe (*A. divaricatum*) were associated with infection of pinyon pine (*Pinus edulis* Engelm.) in northern Arizona by pinyon ips (*Ips confusus*). Millar and others (2005) suggested that an increase in limber pine mortality in the central Sierra Nevada from 1993 to 1998 may have been a response to multiple stressors, including low precipitation, high minimum temperatures, and infection by dwarf mistletoe (*A. cyanocarpum*) and bark beetles.

Assessment and Analysis

Likelihood of increased disease damage—

Warmer, drier—Moderate (moderately certain) (Applicable criteria: a, b).

Warmer, wetter—Moderate (reasonably certain) (Applicable criterion: a).

Increases in temperature will increase dwarf mistletoe survival and host infection. Decreases in precipitation will likely increase host stress, increasing damage from the pathogen. However, extremely dry conditions may result in host mortality, resulting in a decrease in survival and infection of dwarf mistletoe.

As climate changes, the distribution of dwarf mistletoes is expected to follow the shift in distribution of their hosts. Because cold temperatures limit the ranges of many dwarf mistletoes, increases in temperature likely will result in range extensions. Southwestern dwarf mistletoe (*A. vaginatum* ssp. *cryptopodum*) does not occur throughout the entire range of ponderosa pine; distinct northern and upper and lower elevational limits exist (Mark and Hawksworth 1976). The northern and upper elevational limits appear to be related to cold temperatures. Surveys of occurrence, slope association, and severity of infection of several dwarf mistletoe species in Colorado revealed elevational zones specific to each host-parasite interaction (Williams 1971). For example, *A. vaginatum* was absent below 1860 m. Below 2130 m, ponderosa pine is vigorous and may be resistant, with temperature possibly being important. Dwarf mistletoe (*A. americanum*) on lodgepole pine occurs at the lower but not at the upper elevational limits of its host (Hawksworth 1956). The growing season at higher elevations may not be long enough for the fruit of the mistletoe to mature before autumn frosts occur. Although ponderosa pine in the Black Hills is susceptible to dwarf mistletoe infection, dwarf mistletoe is absent from the Black Hills and Bearlodge Mountains, apparently because early onset of the cold season kills young embryos of an essentially tropical mistletoe (Alexander 1987). Bloomberg (1987) suggested that differences in incidence and severity of hemlock dwarf mistletoe (*A. tsugense*) among geographic areas (low in Alaska, moderate to high in British Columbia, and moderate in Washington and Oregon) reflect the effects of climate on seed production and spread, stand composition and growth rate, and local adaptations of dwarf mistletoe. Lodgepole pine dwarf mistletoe is a pathogen of jack pine (*Pinus banksiana* Lamb.) in western Canada, but is absent from jack pine forests in colder, more northern areas (Brandt and others 2004). The distribution of the pathogen may expand if temperatures in Canada's northern interior continue to increase, with a decrease in the frequency of extremely cold periods during the winter, similar to weather over the last several decades.

Consequences of increased disease damage—
High (very certain) (Applicable criteria: a, b, c).

Dwarf mistletoes attack hosts with substantial commercial value, cause tree mortality or predispose their hosts to other disease agents, and reduce host growth.

Risk potential—
Warmer, drier—High (6) (Likelihood of increased disease damage = moderate; consequences of increased pest damage = high).

Warmer, wetter—High (6) (Likelihood of increased disease damage = moderate; consequences of increased disease damage = high).

Warmer temperatures may enable range expansion of some dwarf mistletoes. An increased incidence of summer drought would increase mortality of infected trees.

Armillaria Root Disease

Pathogen—

Armillaria spp.; primarily *Armillaria solidipes* Peck (*Armillaria ostoyae* (Romagnesi) Herink); Agaricales, Marasmiaceae.

Hosts—

Many conifer species, occasionally hardwoods.

Distribution—

Nine species of *Armillaria* are known from North America. Of those, *Armillaria solidipes* causes the greatest damage to conifers in the Western United States and Canada.

History and Current Status

Armillaria species cause root rot in forests worldwide (Kile and others 1991). Some *Armillaria* species are primary pathogens and attack healthy trees in western forests, whereas other species act as secondary agents, infecting after hosts have been stressed by agents such as drought, other diseases, insects, or reductions in habitat quality. Thus, the ecological roles of *Armillaria* species include primary pathogen, secondary invader, and saprotroph. In western North America, *A. solidipes* (*A. ostoyae*) causes disease in conifers (figs. 9 and 10) (Wargo and Shaw 1985). The species is widespread and infects a wide range of hosts (Kile and others 1991).

Economic and Environmental Impacts

Several species of *Armillaria* cause root disease in forest trees, resulting in mortality or reduced growth (Shaw and Kile 1991). In many temperate coniferous forests, *A. solidipes* causes tree mortality throughout a stand's life (Kile and others 1991), ranging from extensive within a disease center to diffuse throughout a stand. In young stands, mortality can reach 2 percent per

Figure 9—Armillaria root disease killing Douglas-fir in clumps near Salmon Arm, British Columbia.

Michael Cruickshank, Natural Resources Canada, Canadian Forest Service

Figure 10—*Armillaria* mushrooms growing near a tree stump near Valemount, British Columbia. Typically *Armillaria* feeds on root systems or colonizes stumps left after harvesting, and then spreads to adjacent trees.

year (Filip and Goheen 1995, Livingston 1990, Morrison and Pellow 1994, Singh and Richardson 1973, Whitney 1988), and cumulative mortality can reach 15 to 20 percent when the stand is 20 years old (Morrison and Pellow 1994, Whitney 1988). Infection can substantially decrease growth in some hosts, especially Douglas-fir and true fir (*Abies* spp.) (Kile and others 1991). Up to 40 percent loss of volume over 4 to 8 years in 18-year-old Douglas-fir, frequently in the absence of aboveground symptoms, has been reported in British Columbia (Cruickshank 2000, Morrison and others 2000). Armillaria root disease caused by *A. solidipes* is responsible for losses in timber volume of 2 to 3 million m^3 per year in Canada's Pacific Northwest (Morrison and Mallett 1996). Tree mortality and subsequent windthrow owing to *Armillaria* decay may be substantial hazards in recreational and urban areas.

Disease Cycle

In general, *Armillaria* decays wood in the roots, lower boles, and stumps of either dead or living trees. Under favorable environmental conditions, the fungus in the infected root—or in the case of the more saprophytic species, in the infested wood—produces mushrooms, the source of the reproductive basidiospores. The mushrooms are produced in clusters of various sizes at the base of dead or dying trees and stumps. These basidiospores are discharged and are carried by air currents to wounds in uninfected trees. The importance of basidiospores in dissemination and infection differs among species (Kile 1986, Smith and others 1992). Local spread from a host tree or stump to an uninfected live tree occurs either by root contact or by rhizomorphs (rootlike fungal structures) that grow through the soil to susceptible tree roots and establish new infections. Most pathogenic species produce limited rhizomorphs and spread primarily through root-to-root contact. Once contact has been made, the fungus spreads along the root system of the uninfected tree, penetrating its bark and entering into the cambium. The fungus continues to spread along the root until it reaches the root collar, where it spreads to the other primary roots. Death of the host occurs when the tree is girdled at the root collar, bark beetles attack, or windthrow occurs. *Armillaria* typically causes a white to yellowish stringy rot. *Armillaria* commonly survives as a saprophyte on dead roots and stumps for 20 to 30 years.

Symptoms of infection in the crown, such as crown thinning, reduced height growth, and distress cone crop, are often unnoticed or similar to other root diseases. Diagnostic signs of *Armillaria* include white mycelial fans under the bark, black rhizomorphs penetrating root surfaces, and honey-colored mushrooms near the base of the tree in autumn.

Environmental Drivers of Disease

Armillaria root disease is often associated with stressed trees (Wargo and Harrington 1991). Stand disturbances such as drought, temperature extremes, and soil compaction reduce host resistance to *Armillaria* (Goheen and Otrosina 1998). *Armillaria* itself makes trees more susceptible to bark beetle attack.

Lack of precipitation decreases trees' resistance to *Armillaria* infection. In general, losses attributed to Armillaria root disease are most severe in Mediterranean or continental interior regions (Kile and others 1991). *Armillaria* occurs most frequently and is most severe in the dry forests of eastern Washington. Whitney (1984) found that conifers were more heavily infected on dry than on wet sites. Morrison and others (2000) found that the percentage of trees showing aboveground symptoms in a dry region was twice that in moist and wet regions. McDonald and others (1987) reported that *Armillaria* species were absent from areas that were relatively warm and dry and cold and wet in national forests of the northern Rocky Mountains.

Although mortality from *A. solidipes* is greater in inland than in coastal forests (Goheen and Otrosina 1998), the pathogen is widespread in both regions (Hadfield and others 1986, Morrison 1981). On coastal sites in British Columbia, *A. solidipes* was prevalent on sites with slightly dry soils, and occurred at low frequency on sites with moist soils. On interior sites, the frequency of *A. solidipes* was lowest on sites with dry soil (Cruickshank and others 1997). In moist north-temperate and boreal coniferous forests, *A. solidipes* causes lethal primary root disease and reduces timber yield (Kile and others 1991). In British Columbia, tree mortality and growth losses attributed to *A. solidipes* were severe throughout the moist southern interior. In addition, Williams and Marsden (1982) found that disease incidence in Idaho was greatest on wet sites with low water retention and on dry sites with high water retention.

Assessment and Analysis

Likelihood of increased disease damage—

Warmer, drier—High (very certain) (Applicable criteria: a, b, d, e).

Warmer, wetter—Moderate (moderately certain) (Applicable criteria: a, d, e).

The incidence of Armillaria root disease is likely to increase as temperatures increase and precipitation decreases (Shaw and Kile 1991, U.S. Office of Technology Assessment 1993), especially when hosts are stressed by moisture deficiency.

Such increases not only will decrease tree growth and increase direct mortality, but may increase the incidence or severity of insect outbreaks on stressed trees (Battles and others 2006). Klopfenstein and others (2009a) projected that the area that can support Douglas-fir in the interior Northwestern United States will decrease in the decade 2060, and suggested that stressed Douglas-fir will be more susceptible to Armillaria root disease.

Armillaria sinapina, typically regarded as a weak pathogen of diverse hosts (Morrison and others 1985), is projected to cause more disease as incidence of stressed hosts increases (Klopfenstein and others 2009b). In the Pacific Northwest, where the mean annual temperature currently is below the optimum (25 °C) for *Armillaria* growth, increases in temperature are likely to result in increased prevalence and rate of spread of root disease (IPCC 2001).

Consequences of increased disease damage—
High (reasonably certain) (Applicable criteria: a, b, c).

As precipitation decreases, increased growth reduction and mortality losses in British Columbia could increase.[4] Increased growth loss and mortality would likely increase as sites become drier elsewhere as well.

Risk potential—
Warmer, drier—Very high (9) (Likelihood of increased disease damage = high; consequences of increased disease damage = high).

Warmer, wetter—High (6) (Likelihood of increased disease damage = moderate; consequences of increased disease damage = high).

A warmer climate will generally increase *Armillaria* incidence and impact as host stress increases. A drier climate would, in general, stress hosts more than a wetter climate, and thus increase host susceptibility.

---

[4] Cruickshank, M.G.; Morrison, D.J. 2003. *Armillaria* mortality and growth loss estimates for interior Douglas-fir in the Interior Cedar-Hemlock ecosystem. Unpublished report. On file with: Canadian Forest Service, Pacific Forestry Centre, 506 West Burnside Road, Victoria, BC V8Z 1M5.

Yellow-Cedar Decline

Pathogen—
Abiotic.

Host—
Yellow-cedar (*Callitropsis* [*Chamaecyparis*] *nootkatensis* (D. Don) Florin.

Distribution—
Southeastern Alaska, northern coastal British Columbia.

History and Current Status

Studies of stand age suggest yellow-cedar decline (fig. 11) began in southeast Alaska around 1880, at the end of several centuries with relatively cool temperatures (Hennon and others 1990a). Yellow-cedar decline was first reported in 1909 (Sheldon 1912). Aerial photographs indicate that, by 1920, large stands of cedar were dead. By the 1970s and 1980s, yellow-cedar mortality was so high that pathologists thought a biotic pathogen was infecting the trees (Hennon and others 1990b). However, no biotic factor appears to be the cause (Hennon and others 1990b).

Yellow-cedar decline is most severe on trees at elevations lower than 300 m in southeast Alaska and British Columbia. Wet soils, an open canopy, and low elevations appear to be associated with decline (Hennon and others 1990a). The decline

Figure 11—Dead Alaska yellow-cedar near Slocum Inlet, Alaska.

Paul Hennon, USDA Forest Service, Pacific Northwest Research Station is believed to result from thaw-freeze damage to roots. As spring temperatures increase and the depth of the snowpack, which insulates roots, decreases, roots deharden prematurely and are susceptible to injury and death following spring freezes (Hennon and others 2006, Klinka and others 2000, Schaberg and others 2008).

The initial symptom of yellow-cedar decline is death of fine roots. Trees that lose rootlets fade, have thin or off-color crowns, and develop necrotic lesions on large roots. Infested stands may have numerous standing dead trees, some that died recently and others that died as much as 100 years ago (Hennon and Shaw 1997). Snags may remain standing for many years because yellow-cedar heartwood decomposes slowly (Barton 1976). As the number of standing dead trees increases, more than 70 percent of the basal area of yellow-cedar may be dead (Hennon and others 2005).

Decline of yellow-cedar has occurred on 200 000 ha of temperate rain forests across southeastern Alaska (Beier and others 2008, Snyder 2005) and northern coastal British Columbia (Hennon and others 2005). In Alaska, concentrated mortality occurs in a wide band from western Chichagof and the Baranof Islands to the Ketchikan area. Ground surveys show that in this band, 65 percent of the basal area of yellow-cedar is dead (USDA FS 1999). The distribution of decline parallels milder winter temperature isoclines in the region (Hennon and Shaw 1994). The total area affected by yellow-cedar decline has been increasing quite gradually (less than 1 m per year). Most stands contain dead trees; dying cedars with yellow, red, or thinning crowns; healthy cedars; and other tree species (USDA FS 1999).

Economic and Environmental Impacts

The economic value of dead yellow-cedar is high, but the trees often are not harvested. Accordingly, economic impacts appear to be minimal. Yellow-cedar decline alters stand structure by increasing the number of snags and alters stand composition as other trees replace the yellow-cedar. Over time, stands are dominated by other conifer species (USDA FS 1999). Growth of trees that co-occur with yellow-cedar may increase if competition with yellow-cedar decreases. Growth of other species of trees also may decrease, and mortality increase, on sites with poor drainage. Stands in which yellow-cedar decline has been present for the past century increasingly are dominated by western hemlock (*Tsuga heterophylla* (Raf.) Sarg.) and mountain hemlock (*Tsuga mertensiana* (Bong.) Carr). Accumulation of understory biomass of shrubs also is increasing considerably in some of these stands (USDA FS 1999).

The presence of yellow-cedar decline in southeast Alaska was associated with a 3.8-fold increase in the frequency of landslides compared to unaffected slopes because soil was prone to erosion (Johnson and Wilcock 2002).

Environmental Drivers of Disease

Yellow-cedar decline is caused by a reduction in depth of spring snowpack at lower elevations. Snow acts like a blanket on the ground, maintaining the soil and fine cedar rootlets at a consistent temperature. The trees continue to thrive at higher elevations where deep snowpack minimizes the probability that roots will freeze during the early spring.

Assessment and Analysis

Because yellow-cedar decline is caused by abiotic factors, criteria related to biology, such as reproduction, spread, infection, and reproductive potential, are not applicable. Assessment was based on the remaining criteria.

Likelihood of increased disease damage—

Warmer, drier—Moderate (reasonably certain) (Applicable criteria: b, e).

Warmer, wetter—Low (reasonably certain) (Applicable criterion: e).

If temperature continues to increase and precipitation and depth of snowpack continues to decline, yellow-cedar decline may expand to higher elevations. This type of expansion has been observed at a few sites in southeast Alaska (Beier 2006, Beier and others 2008). If snowfall increases, the roots may be protected, and hosts will be less stressed despite increases in temperature; therefore, criterion b would not apply.

Consequences of increased disease damage—

High (moderately certain) (Applicable criteria: a, b, d, e).

Lower elevation forests may undergo changes in tree species composition. The economic value of dead yellow-cedar is high, but few trees currently are salvaged. Trees will persist at higher elevations where temperatures are relatively low and snow cover protects roots from freezing. Yellow-cedar has a limited natural distribution.

Risk potential—

Warmer, drier—High (6) (Likelihood of increased disease damage = moderate; consequences of increased disease damage = high).

Warmer, wetter—Moderate (3) (Likelihood of increased disease damage = low; consequences of increased pest damage = high).

Continued warming would likely increase mortality of yellow-cedar. The resulting economic and environmental loss rates are potentially high, but would depend on whether the trees are salvaged for value.

Summary and Conclusions

This risk assessment of climate change projected the effects of eight forest diseases under two climate-change scenarios (tables 3 and 4).

Table 3—Risk potentials for selected diseases given projected increases in temperature and decreases in precipitation by 2100

Disease	Likelihood of increased disease damage	Consequences of increased disease damage	Risk potential
Dothistroma needle blight	Low (1)	Moderate (2)	Low (2)
Swiss needle cast	Low (1)	Moderate (2)	Low (2)
Sudden oak death/ramorum blight	Low (1)	High (3)	Moderate (3)
White pine blister rust	Low (1)	High (3)	Moderate (3)
Cytospora canker of alder	High (3)	Moderate (2)	High (6)
Dwarf mistletoes	Moderate (2)	High (3)	High (6)
Armillaria root disease	High (3)	High (3)	Very high (9)
Yellow-cedar decline	Moderate (2)	High (3)	High (6)

Table 4—Risk potentials for selected diseases given projected increases in temperature and precipitation by 2100

Disease	Likelihood of increased disease damage	Consequences of increased disease damage	Risk potential
Dothistroma needle blight	Moderate (2)	Moderate (2)	Moderate (4)
Swiss needle cast	Moderate (2)	Moderate (2)	Moderate (4)
Sudden oak death/ramorum blight	High(3)	High (3)	Very high (3)
White pine blister rust	Low (1)	High (3)	Moderate (3)
Cytospora canker of alder	Moderate (2)	Moderate (2)	Moderate (4)
Dwarf mistletoes	Moderate (2)	High (3)	High (6)
Armillaria root disease	Moderate (2)	High (3)	High (6)
Yellow-cedar decline	Low (1)	High (3)	Moderate (3)

Because most foliar pathogens, including *P. ramorum*, require moisture for sporulation, dissemination, and infection, decreases in precipitation generally will decrease the likelihood of disease damage. Some needle cast diseases caused by species of *Davisomycella* and *Hypodermella* also require moisture for sporulation, dispersal, and infection, but are more likely to infect trees that are stressed by drought (Worrall and Sullivan 2002).

The biology of stem rust pathogens on two-needled and three-needle pines in western North America—for example, western gall rust (*Endocronartium harknessii*), comandra rust (*Cronartium comandrae*), stalactiform rust (*C. coleosporioides*), and sweet fern rust (*C. comptoniae*)—is similar to *C. ribicola*. Infection and incidence of diseases caused by these fungi generally increases when conditions are cool and moist. The risk potential of these rusts likely is similar to that of white pine blister rust. Warmer conditions, whether wetter or drier, would be less favorable than cooler conditions.

The risk potentials for *Cytospora* canker of alder could be extrapolated to other stress-related canker diseases. Most canker diseases are caused by facultative parasites such as *Botryosphaeria*, *Sphaeropsis*, *Cytospora*, and *Biscogniauxia* (*Hypoxylon*) (Desprez-Loustau and others 2006). These fungi are more likely to cause damage to trees that are stressed by heat and drought (Lonsdale and Gibbs 2002; Schoeneweiss 1975, 1981). Not all canker diseases are associated with stressed hosts. The incidence of some canker pathogens, such as *Thyronectria austro-americana* on honeylocust (*Gleditsia triacanthos* L.) and *Cryphonectria cubensis* on *Eucalyptus* spp., is associated with high rainfall, and their hosts display some resistance to drought stress (Desprez-Loustau and others 2006).

The root pathogen *Armillaria* is more successful when hosts are stressed by drought. A root disease similar to *Armillaria*, Heterobasidion root disease, may also have a higher risk potential as temperature increases and precipitation decreases. In North America, *Heterobadision irregulare* and *H. occidentale*—formerly the intersterility groups P and S, respectively, of *H. annosum* (Otrosina and Garbelotto 2010)—cause substantial wood decay (Goheen and Otrosina 1998). Host stress, in particular soil moisture stress (Towers and Stambaugh 1968), increases host susceptibility to *Heterobadision*. Infection and damage in coniferous forests is lowest when temperatures are low and precipitation is high (Shaw 1988). In the southeastern United States, Heterobasidion root disease is more prevalent in sandy, dry soils than in heavier soils with poor drainage or high water tables (Froelich and others 1966, Kuhlman and others 1976).

The criteria used here to determine likelihood of increased disease damage are not entirely appropriate for a strictly abiotic disease such as yellow-cedar decline. The criteria for consequences of increased damage apply, but the criteria for likelihood of increase damage include two (a and c) relating to pathogen biology that do not.

Although the results of this risk assessment suggest that climate change will affect forest health, the uncertainties associated with the risk potentials should be kept in mind. In this assessment, uncertainty arises regarding the degree of climate change that will occur, pathogen biology under changing climate; the effects of changing climate directly on the host, and the interactions between the pathogen, host, and climate.

The information provided in this risk assessment should be useful to decision-makers and managers for strategic and management planning, the second step in a risk analysis. This risk assessment also serves as the basis for subsequent communication instruments or products for audiences in addition to technical users. The communication of the risk assessment, the third step in a risk analysis, can have different written and oral forms to meet the needs of the intended audiences (e.g., risk managers, the public).

Acknowledgments

This risk assessment is the result of the "Climate Change and Western Forest Diseases" project sponsored by the USDA FS Western Wildland Environmental Threat Assessment Center (WWETAC) and the Pacific Southwest Research Station (PSW). The project builds on a June 2007 workshop on climate change and forest insects and diseases held by WWETAC (Beukema and others 2007) in October 2007 that was sponsored by the USDA FS, WWETAC, and PSW in cooperation with the 2007 Western International Forest Disease Work Conference, and a literature review of climate change and forest diseases in western North America (Kliejunas and others 2009). The author appreciates the reviews and assistance of Susan Frankel, USDA FS, PSW; Jeff Hicke, USDA FS WWETAC; James Worrall, USDA FS, Forest Health Protection, Rocky Mountain Region; and Erica Fleishman, University of California, Santa Barbara.

English Equivalents

When you know:	Multiply by:	To find:
Millimeters (mm)	0.0394	Inches
Centimeters (cm)	0.394	Inches
Kilometers (km)	0.621	Miles
Meters (m)	3.28	Feet
Hectares (ha)	2.47	Acres (ac)
Cubic meters (cm^3)	35.314	Cubic feet (ft^3)
Degrees Celsius (°C)	1.8 and add 32	Degrees Fahrenheit

Literature Cited

Ades, P.K.; Simpson, J.A.; Eldridge, K.G.; Eldridge, R.H. 1992. Genetic variation in susceptibility to Dothistroma needle blight among provenances and families of *Pinus muricata*. Canadian Journal of Forest Research. 22: 111–117.

Alexander, R.R. 1987. Silvicultural systems, cutting methods, and cultural practices for Black Hills ponderosa pine. Gen. Tech. Rep. RM-139. Fort Collins, CO: U.S. Department of Agriculture, Forest Service, Rocky Mountain Forest and Range Experiment Station. 32 p.

Archer, S.R.; Predick, K. 2008a. Climate change and ecosystems of the southwestern United States. Rangelands. 30: 23–28.

Archer, S.R.; Predick, K. 2008b. Understanding the problem of climate change and western ecosystems: considerations and tools for ecoregional assessment. A review of current literature. http://www.blm.gov/pgdata/etc/medialib/blm/wy/programs/science.Par.23352.File.dat/ClimateChange-EcoregionalAssessment.pdf. (June 2011).

Archibald, S.; Brown, A. 2007. The relationship between climate and incidence of red band needle blight in the East Anglia forest district, Britain. Acta Silvatica et Lignaria Hungarica Special Edition: 260.

Arno, S.F. 2000. Fire in western forest ecosystems. In: Brown, J.K.; Smith, J.K., eds. Wildland fire in ecosystems: effects of fire on flora. Gen. Tech. Rep. RMRS-GTR-42. Ogden, UT: U.S. Department of Agriculture, Forest Service, Rocky Mountain Research Station: 97–120.

Barnes, I.; Crous, P.W.; Wingfield, B.D.; Wingfield, M.J. 2004. Multigene phylogenies reveal that red band needle blight is caused by two distinct species of *Dothistroma*, *D. septosporum* and *D. pini*. Studies in Mycology. 50: 551–565.

Bartlein, P.J.; Whitlock, C.; Shafer, S.F. 1997. Future climate in the Yellowstone National Park region and its potential impact on vegetation. Conservation Biology. 11: 782–792.

Barton, G.M. 1976. A review of yellow-cedar (*Chamaecyparis nootkatensis* [D. Don] Spach) extractives and their importance to utilization. Wood and Fiber. 8: 172–176.

Battles, J.J.; Robards, T.; Das, A.; Waring, K.; Gilless, J.K.; Schurr, F.; LeBlanc, J.; Biging, G.; Simon, C. 2006. Climate change impact on forest resources. A report from: California Climate Change Center. CEC-500-2005-193-SF. 45 p. http://www.energy.ca.gov/2005publications/CEC-500-2005-193/CEC-500-2005-193-SF.PDF. (June 2011).

Bega, R.V. 1960. The effect of environment on germination of sporidia of *Cronartium ribicola*. Phytopathology. 50: 61–68.

Bega, R.V. 1978. Rusts. In: Bega, R.V., tech. coord. Diseases of Pacific Coast conifers. Agric. Handb. 521. Washington, DC: U.S. Department of Agriculture, Forest Service, Government Printing Office: 91–120.

Beier, C. 2006. Widespread decline of yellow-cedar and climatic change in southeastern Alaska. Global glimpses, Center for Global Change and Arctic System Research. 14(1): 7–8.

Beier, C.M.; Sink, S.E.; Hennon, P.E.; D'Amore, D.V.; Juday, G.P. 2008. Twentieth-century warming and the dendroclimatology of declining yellow-cedar forests in southeastern Alaska. Canadian Journal of Forest Research. 38: 1319–1334.

Beukema, S.J.; Robinson, D.C.E.; Greig, L.A. 2007. Forests, insects & pathogens and climate change: workshop report. Prepared for The Western Wildlands Environmental Threat Assessment Center, Prineville, Oregon. 20 p. + appendices. http://www.essa.com/documents/Forests,%20Pests%20and%20Climate%20-%20Workshop%20Report.pdf. (June 2011).

Bingham, R.T.; Hoff, R.J.; McDonald, G.I. 1971. Disease resistance in forest trees. Annual Review of Phytopathology. 9: 433–454.

Black, B.A.; Shaw, D.C.; Stone, J.K. 2010. Impacts of Swiss needle cast on overstory Douglas-fir forests of the western Oregon Coast Range. Forest Ecology and Management. 259(8): 1673–1680.

Bloomberg, W.J. 1987. Comparison of dwarf mistletoe effects on hemlock in Alaska, British Columbia and the Pacific Northwest. In: 34th western international forest disease work conference. [Place of publication unknown]: [Publisher unknown]: 35–40.

Boland, G.J.; Melzer, M.S.; Hopkin, A.; Higgins, V.; Nassuth, A. 2004. Climate change and plant diseases in Ontario. Canadian Journal of Plant Pathology. 26: 335–350.

Boyce, J.S. 1940. A needle-cast of Douglas-fir associated with *Adelopus gaeumannii*. Phytopathology. 30: 649–659.

Bradshaw, R.E. 2004. Dothistroma (red-band) needle blight of pines and the dothistromin toxin: a review. Forest Pathology. 34: 1631–1685.

Bradshaw, R.E.; Ganley, R.J.; Jones, W.T.; Dyer, P.S. 2000. High levels of dothistromin toxin produced by the forest pathogen *Dothistroma pini*. Mycological Research. 104: 325–332.

Brandt, J.P.; Hiratsuka, Y.; Pluth, D.J. 2004. Extreme cold temperatures and survival of overwintering and germinated *Arceuthobium americanum* seeds. Canadian Journal of Forest Research. 34: 174–183.

Brasier, C.; Denman, S.; Brown, A.; Webber, J.F. 2004. Sudden oak death (*Phytophthora ramorum*) discovered on trees in Europe. Mycological Research. 108: 1107–1110.

Brasier, C.; Denman, S.; Webber, J.; Brown, A. 2006. Sudden oak death: recent developments on trees in Europe. In: Frankel, S.J.; Shea, P.J.; Haverty, M.I., tech. coords. Proceedings, sudden oak death second science symposium: the state of our knowledge. Gen. Tech. Rep. PSW-GTR-196. Albany, CA: U.S. Department of Agriculture, Forest Service, Pacific Southwest Research Station: 31–33.

Brown, A.V.; Rose, D.R.; Webber, J.F. 2003. Red band needle blight of pine. Forest Research Information Note 49. Edinburgh, United Kingdom: UK Forestry Commission.

Brown, A.V.; Webber, J.F. 2008. Red band needle blight of conifers in Britain. Forestry Commission Research Note 002. Edinburgh, United Kingdom: UK Forestry Commission. 8 p.

Bulman, L.S. 1993. Cyclaneusma needle cast and Dothistroma needle blight in NZ pine plantations. New Zealand Forestry. 38: 21–24.

Bulman, L.S. 2008. Dothistroma needle blight. Forest Pathology in New Zealand No. 5. http://www.nzffa.org.nz/farm-forestry-model/the-essentials/forest-health-pests-and-diseases/diseases/Needle-diseases/. (June 2011).

Bulman, L.; Ganley, R.; Dick, M. 2008. Needle diseases of radiata pine in New Zealand. Client Report No. 13010. 81 p.

Byler, J.W. 1978. The pest damage inventory in California. In: Scharpf, R.F.; Parmeter, J.R., Jr., tech. coords. Proceedings of the symposium on dwarf mistletoe control through forest management. Gen. Tech. Rep. PSW-031. Berkeley, CA: U.S. Department of Agriculture, Forest Service, Pacific Southwest Research Station: 162–171.

Campbell, E.M.; Antos, J.A. 2000. Distribution and severity of white pine blister rust and mountain pine beetle on whitebark pine in British Columbia. Canadian Journal of Forest Research. 30: 1051–1059.

Cave, G.L.; Randall-Schadel, B.R.; Redlin, S.C. 2008. Risk analysis for *Phytophthora ramorum* Werres, de Cock & In't Veld, causal agent of *Phytophthora* canker (sudden oak death), ramorum leaf blight, and ramorum dieback. November 19, 2007 Revision 1. Raleigh, NC: U.S. Department of Agriculture, Animal and Plant Health Inspection Service, Plant Protection and Quarantine. 88 p.

Cayan, D.; Luers, A.; Hanemann, M.; Franco, G. 2006. Scenarios of climate change in California: an overview. California Climate Change Center-California Energy Commission. Publication No. CEC-500-2005-186-SF. 47 p. http://www.energy.ca.gov/2005publications/CEC-500-2005-186/CEC-500-2005-186-SF.PDF. (June 2011).

Chambers, J.C.; Pellant, M. 2008. Climate change impacts on northwestern and intermountain United States rangelands. Rangelands. 30: 29–33.

Childs, T.W. 1960. Drought effects on conifers in the Pacific Northwest, 1958–59. Res. Note PNW–182. Portland, OR: U.S. Department of Agriculture, Forest Service, Pacific Northwest Forest and Range Experiment Station. 5 p.

Craig, G.A. 1979. Integrated forest pest management as seen by a forest land owner. In: Executive summaries; proceedings 1978 western forestry conference. [Place of publication unknown]: Western Forestry Conservation Association: 61.

Cruickshank, M. 2000. Volume loss of Douglas-fir infected with *Armillaria ostoyae*. In: Hellstedt, C.; Sutherland, K.; Innes, T., eds. Proceedings: From science to management and back: a science forum for southern interior ecosystems of British Columbia. Kamloops, BC: Southern Interior Forest Extension and Research Partnership: 127–129.

Cruickshank, M.G.; Morrison, D.J.; Punja, Z.K. 1997. Incidence of *Armillaria* species in precommercial thinning stumps and spread of *Armillaria ostoyae* to adjacent Douglas-fir trees. Canadian Journal of Forest Research. 27: 481–490.

Davidson, J.M.; Rizzo, D.M.; Garbelotto, M.; Tjosvold, S.; Slaughter, G.W. 2002. *Phytophthora ramorum* and sudden oak death in California. II. Transmission and survival. In: Standiford, R.B.; McCreary, D.; Purcell, K.L., tech. coords. Proceedings of the fifth symposium on oak woodlands: oaks in California's changing landscape. Gen. Tech. Rep. PSW-GTR-184. Albany, CA: U.S. Department of Agriculture, Forest Service, Pacific Southwest Research Station: 741–749.

Davidson, J.M.; Wickland, A.C.; Patterson, H.A.; Falk, K.R.; Rizzo, D.M. 2005. Transmission of *Phytophthora ramorum* in mixed evergreen forest in California. Phytopathology. 95: 587–596.

Desprez-Loustau, M-L.; Marcais, B.; Nageleisen, L.M.; Ouiym, D.; Vannini, A. 2006. Interactive effects of drought and pathogens in forest trees. Annals of Forest Science. 63(6): 597.

Desprez-Loustau, M-L.; Robin, C.; Reynaud, G.; Deque, M.; Badeau, V.; Piou, D.; Husson, C.; Marcais, B. 2007. Simulating the effects of a climate-change scenario on the geographical range and activity of forest pathogenic fungi. Canadian Journal of Plant Pathology. 29: 101–120.

Dettinger, M.D.; Cayan, D.R.; Knowles, N.; Westerling, A.; Tyree, M.K. 2004. Recent projections of 21st-century climate change and watershed responses in the Sierra Nevada. In: Murphy, D.D.; Stine, P.A., eds. Proceedings of the Sierra Nevada science symposium. Gen. Tech. Rep. PSW-GTR-193. Albany, CA: U.S. Department of Agriculture, Forest Service, Pacific Southwest Research Station: 43–46.

Doroguine, G. 1911. Une maladie cryptogamique du pin. Bulletin de la Societe Mycologique deFrance. 27: 105–106.

Downing, M.; O'Brien, J. 2004. ExFor (Exotic Forest Pest Information System for North America). Participant's guidelines. 21 p. http://spfnic.fs.fed.us/exfor/docs/guidelines.pdf. (June 2011).

Drummond, D.B., ed. 1982. Timber loss estimates for the coniferous forests in the United States due to dwarf mistletoes. Rep. 83–2. Fort Collins, CO: U.S. Department of Agriculture, Forest Service, Forest Pest Management, Methods Application Group. 24 p.

Dukes, J.S.; Pontius, J.; Orwig, D.; Garnas, J.R.; Rodgers, V.L.; Brazee, N.; Cooke, B.; Theoharides, K.A.; Stange, E.E.; Harrington, R.; Ehrenfeld, J.; Gurevitch, J.; Lerdau, M.; Stinson, K.; Wick, R.; Ayres, M. 2009. Responses of insect pests, pathogens, and invasive plant species to climate change in the forests of northeastern North America: What can we predict? Canadian Journal of Forest Research. 39: 231–248.

Endangered Species Act of 1973 [ESA]; 16 U.S.C. 15311–1536, 1538–1540.

Environmental Protection Agency. [EPA]. 1992. Risk assessment forum. Framework for ecological risk assessment. Washington, DC: EPA 630/R-92/001.

European and Mediterranean Plant Protection Organization and CAB International. [EPPO and CABI]. 1997. Quarantine pests for Europe. 2nd ed. In: Smith, I.M.; McNamara, D.G.; Scott, P.R.; Holderness, M., eds. Wallingford, United Kingdom: CABI International. 1425 p.

Filip, G.M.; Goheen, D.J. 1995. Precommercial thinning in *Pseudotsuga*, *Tsuga*, and *Abies* stands affected by Armillaria root disease: 10-year results. Canadian Journal of Forest Research. 25: 817–823.

Food and Agriculture Organization and World Health Organization [FAO and WHO]. 1995. Application of risk analysis to food standards issues, a joint FAO/WHO expert consultation. Geneva, Switzerland.

Frankel, S.J. 2008. Sudden oak death and *Phytophthora ramorum* in the USA: a management challenge. Australasian Plant Pathology. 37: 19–25.

Frankel, S.; Denitto, G.; Hart, D. 1988. An evaluation of tree mortality in the Sayles summer home tract, Placerville Ranger District, Eldorado National Forest. For. Pest Mgmt. Rep. 88-19. San Francisco, CA: U.S. Department of Agriculture, Forest Service, Pacific Southwest Region. 17 p.

Froelich, R.C.; Dell, T.R.; Walkinshaw, C.H. 1966. Soil factors associated with *Fomes annosus* in the Gulf States. Forest Science. 12: 356–361.

Gadgil, P.D. 1974. Effect of temperature and leaf wetness period on infection of *Pinus radiata* by *Dothistroma pini*. New Zealand Journal of Forest Science. 4: 495–501.

Gadgil, P.D. 1977. Duration of leaf wetness periods and infection of *Pinus radiata* by *Dothistroma pini*. New Zealand Journal of Forest Science. 7: 83–90.

Garbelotto, M.; Davidson, J.M.; Ivors, K.; Maloney, P.E.; Hüberli, D.; Koike, S.T.; Rizzo, D.M. 2003. Non-oak native plants are main hosts for sudden oak death pathogen in California. California Agriculture. 57: 18–23.

Garbelotto, M.; Rizzo, D.M. 2005. A California-based chronological review (1995–2004) of research on *Phytophthora ramorum*, the causal agent of sudden oak death. Phytopathologia Mediterranea. 44(2): 127–144.

Garfin, G.; Eischeid, J.; Lenart, M.; Cole, K.; Ironside, K.; Cobb, N. 2010. Downscaling climate projection in topographically diverse landscapes of the Colorado Plateau in the arid southwestern United States. In: Van Riper, C., III; Wakeling, B.F.; Sisk, T.D., eds. The Colorado Plateau IV. Tucson, AZ: University of Arizona Press: 21-44.

Geils, B.W.; Cibrian-Tovar, J.; Moody, B., tech. coords. 2002. Mistletoes of North American conifers. Gen. Tech. Rep. RMRS-GTR-98. Ogden, UT: U.S. Department of Agriculture, Forest Service, Rocky Mountain Research Station. 123 p.

Geils, B.W.; Hawksworth, F.G. 2002. Damage, effects, and importance of dwarf mistletoes. In: Geils, B.W.; Cibrian-Tovar, J.; Moody, B., tech. coords. Mistletoes of North American conifers. Gen. Tech. Rep. RMRS-GTR-98. Ogden, UT: U.S. Department of Agriculture, Forest Service, Rocky Mountain Research Station: 57–65.

Gibson, I.A.S. 1972. Dothistroma blight of *Pinus radiata*. Annual Review of Phytopathology. 10: 51–72.

Gibson, I.A.S. 1974. Impact and control of Dothistroma blight of pines. European Journal of Forest Pathology. 4: 89–100.

Gibson, I.A.S.; Christensen, P.S.; Munga, F.N. 1964. First observations in Kenya on a foliage disease of pines, caused by *Dothistroma pini* Hulbary. Commonwealth Forestry Review. 43: 31–48.

Gibson, K.E.; Skov, K.; Kegley, S.; Jorgensen, C.; Smith, S.; Witcosky, J. 2008. Mountain pine beetle impacts in high elevation five needle pines: current trends and challenges. Rep. R1-08-020. Missoula, MT: U.S. Department of Agriculture, Forest Service, Northern Region, Forest Health Protection. 32 p.

Goheen, D.J.; Otrosina, W.J. 1998. Characteristics and consequences of root diseases in forests of western North America. Gen. Tech. Rep. PSW-GTR-165. Berkeley, CA: U.S. Department of Agriculture, Forest Service, Pacific Southwest Research Station: 3–8.

Groenewald, M.; Barnes, I.; Bradshaw, R.E.; Brown A.V.; Dale, A.; Groenewald, J.Z.; Lewis, K.J.; Wingfield, B.D.; Wingfield, M.J.; Crous, P.W. 2007. Characterization and distribution of mating type genes in the Dothistroma needle blight pathogens. Phytopathology. 97: 825–834.

Grünwald, N.J.; Goss, E.M.; Larsen, M.M.; Press, C.M.; McDonald, V.T.; Blomquist, C.L.; Thomas, S.L. 2008a. First report of the European lineage of *Phytophthora ramorum* on *Viburnum* and *Osmanthus* spp. in a California nursery. Plant Disease. 92: 314.

Grünwald, N.J.; Goss, E.M.; Press, C.M. 2008b. *Phytophthora ramorum*: a pathogen with a remarkably wide host range causing sudden oak death on oaks and ramorum blight on woody ornamentals. Molecular Plant Pathology. 9: 729–740.

Hadfield, J.S.; Goheen, D.J.; Filip, G.M.; Schmitt, C.L.; Harvey, R.D. 1986. Root diseases in Washington and Oregon conifers. R6-FPM-250-86, Portland, OR: U.S. Department of Agriculture, Forest Service, State and Private Forestry, Forest Pest Management. 27 p.

Hamann, A.; Wang, T. 2006. Potential effects of climate change on ecosystem and tree species distribution in British Columbia. Ecology. 87: 2773–2786.

Hansen, E.M.; Kanaskie, A.; Prospero, S.; McWilliams, M.; Goheen, E.M.; Osterbauer, N.; Reeser, P.; Sutton, W. 2008. Epidemiology of *Phytophthora ramorum* in Oregon tanoak forests. Canadian Journal of Forest Research. 38: 1133–1143.

Hansen, E.M.; Stone, J.K.; Capitano, B.R.; Rosso, P.; Sutton, W.; Winton, L.; Kanaskie, A.; McWilliams, M.G. 2000. Incidence and impact of Swiss needle cast in forest plantations of Douglas-fir in coastal Oregon. Plant Disease. 84: 773–778.

Hansen, E.; Sutton, W.; Parke, J.; Linderman, R. 2002. *Phytophthora ramorum* and Oregon forest trees—one pathogen, three diseases. In: Proceedings of the sudden oak death science symposium. Berkeley, CA: U.S. Department of Agriculture, Forest Service and University of California, Berkeley.

Hawksworth, F.G. 1956. Upper altitudinal limits of lodgepole pine dwarf mistletoe in the central Rocky Mountains. Phytopathology. 46: 561–562.

Hawksworth, F.G.; Wiens, D. 1970. Biology and taxonomy of the dwarf mistletoes. Annual Review of Phytopathology. 8: 187–208.

Hawksworth, F.G.; Weins, D., eds. 1996. Dwarf mistletoes: biology, pathology and systematics. Agric. Handb. 709. Washington, DC: U.S. Department of Agriculture, Forest Service. 410 p.

Hennon, P.E.; D'Amore, D.V.; Wittwer, D.; Johnson, A.; Schaberg, P.; Hawley, G.; Beier, C.; Sink, S.; Juday, G. 2006. Climate warming, reduced snow, and freezing injury could explain the demise of yellow-cedar in southeast Alaska, USA. World Resource Review. 18: 427–450.

Hennon, P.E.; D'Amore, D.; Zeglen, S.; Grainger, M. 2005. Yellow-cedar decline in the north coast forest district of British Colombia. Res. Note PNW-RN-549. Portland, OR: U.S. Department of Agriculture, Forest Service. Pacific Northwest Research Station. 16 p.

Hennon, P.E.; Shaw, C.G., III. 1994. Did climatic warming trigger the onset and development of yellow-cedar decline in southeast Alaska? European Journal of Forest Pathology. 24: 399–418.

Hennon, P.E.; Shaw, C.G., III. 1997. The enigma of yellow-cedar decline: What is killing these long-lived, defensive trees? Journal of Forestry. 95: 4–10.

Hennon, P.E.; Shaw, C.G., III; Hansen, E.M. 1990a. Dating decline and mortality of *Chamaecyparis nootkatensis* in southeast Alaska. Forest Science. 36: 502–515.

Hennon, P.E.; Shaw, C.G., III; Hansen, E.M. 1990b. Symptoms and fungal associations of declining *Chamaecyparis nootkatensis* in southeast Alaska. Plant Disease. 74: 267–273.

Hoff, R.J. 1985. Susceptibility of lodgepole pine to the needle cast fungus *Lophodermella concolor.* Res. Note INT-349. Ogden, UT: U.S. Department of Agriculture, Forest Service, Intermountain Experiment Station. 6 p.

Hood, I.A. 1982. *Phaeocryptopus gaeumannii* on *Pseudotsuga menziesii* in southern British Columbia. New Zealand Journal of Forest Science. 12: 415–424.

Hunt, R.S. 2005. Effect of plant age and length of growing season on the development of blister rust cankers in western white pine. Canadian Journal of Plant Pathology. 27: 453–457.

Intergovernmental Panel on Climate Change [IPCC]. 2001. Chapter 5: Ecosystems and their goods and services/ 5.6.2.2.2. Pressures from diseases and insect herbivory. http://www.grida.no/climate/IPCC_tar/wg2/pdf/ wg2TARchap5.pdf. (June 2011).

Intergovernmental Panel on Climate Change. [IPCC]. 2007. Summary for policy makers. In: Solomon, S.; Qin, D.; Manning, M.; Chen, Z.; Marquis, M.; Averyt, K.B.; Tignor, M.; Miller, H.L., eds. Climate change 2007: the physical science basis. New York: Cambridge University Press.

Ivors, K.; Garbelotto, M.; Vries, I.D.E.; Ruyter-Spira, C.; Heckkert, B.T.E.; Rosenzweig, N.; Bonants, P. 2006. Microsatellite markers identify three lineages of *Phytophthora ramorum* in US nurseries, yet single lineages in US forest and European nursery populations. Molecular Ecology. 15: 1493–1505.

Ivory, M.H. 1967. A new variety of *Dothistroma pini* in Kenya. Transactions of the British Mycological Society. 50: 289–297.

Ivory, M.H. 1972. Infection of *Pinus radiata* foliage by *Scirrhia pini*. Transactions of the British Mycological Society. 59: 205–212.

Jenkinson, J.L. 1990. *Pinus jeffreyi* Grev. and Balf. Jeffrey pine. In: Silvics of North America. Vol. 2 Conifers. Agric. Handb. 654. Washington, DC: U.S. Department of Agriculture, Forest Service: 359–369.

Johnson, A.C.; Wilcock, P. 2002. Association between cedar decline and hillslope stability in mountainous regions of southeast Alaska. Geomorphology. 46: 129–142.

Johnson, G.R.; Grotta, A.T.; Gartner, B.L.; Downes, G. 2005. Impact of the foliar pathogen Swiss needle cast on wood quality of Douglas-fir. Canadian Journal of Forest Research. 35: 331–339.

Kanaskie, A.; Goheen, E.; Osterbauer, N.; McWilliams, M.; Hansen, E.; Sutton, W. 2008. Eradication of *Phytophthora ramorum* from Oregon forests: status after six years. In: Frankel, S.J.; Kliejunas, J.T.; Palmieri, K.M., tech. coords. Proceedings of the sudden oak death third science symposium. Gen. Tech. Rep. PSW-GTR-214. Albany, CA: U.S. Department of Agriculture, Forest Service, Pacific Southwest Research Station: 15–17.

Karadzic, D. 1989. *Scirrhia pini* Funk et Parker. Life cycle of the fungus in plantations of *Pinus nigra* Arn. in Serbia. European Journal of Forest Pathology. 19: 231–236.

Karl, T.R.; Melillo, J.M.; Peterson, T.C.; Hassol, S.J., eds. 2009. Global climate change impacts in the United States. New York, NY: Cambridge University Press. http://www.globalchange.gov/. (June 2011).

Kegley, S.; Schwandt, J.; Gibson, K. 2004. Forest health assessment of whitebark pine in selected stands in the Selkirk Mountain of northern Idaho. Rep. 04-5. Missoula, MT: U.S. Department of Agriculture, Forest Service, Northern Region. 8 p.

Kepley, J.B.; Jacobi, W.R. 2000. Pathogenicity of *Cytospora* fungi and six hardwood species. Journal of Arboriculture. 26: 326–332.

Kessel, G.; Werres, S.; Webber, J. 2007. *P. ramorum* infection process in selected trees and ornamental plants. EU Sixth Framework Project, RAPRA. Deliverable Report 8. http://rapra.csl.gov.uk.

Kile, G.A. 1986. Genotypes of *Armillaria hinnulea* in wet scherophyll eucalypt forest in Tasmania. Transactions of the British Mycological Society. 87: 312–314.

Kile, G.A.; McDonald, G.I.; Byler, J.W. 1991. Ecology and disease in natural forests. In: Shaw, C.G., III; Kile, G.A., eds. Armillaria root disease. Agric. Handb. 691, Washington, DC: U.S. Department of Agriculture: 102–121.

Kimmey, J.W.; Wagener, W.W. 1961. Spread of white pine blister rust from *Ribes* to sugar pine in California and Oregon. Tech. Bull. 1251. Washington, DC: U.S. Department of Agriculture, Forest Service. 71 p.

Kinloch, B.B., Jr. 2003. White pine blister rust in North America: past and prognosis. Phytopathology. 93: 1044–1047.

Kinloch, B.B., Jr.; Dulitz, D.J. 1990. White pine blister rust at Mountain Home Demonstration State Forest: a case study of the epidemic and prospects for genetic control. Res. Pap. PSW-204. Berkeley, CA: U.S. Department of Agriculture, Forest Service, Pacific Southwest Research Station. 7 p.

Kliejunas, J.T.; Burdsall, H.H., Jr.; DeNitto, G.A.; Eglitis, A.; Haugen, D.A.; Harverty, M.I.; Micales, J.A.; Tkacz, B.M.; Powell, M.R. 2003. Pest risk assessment of the importation into the United States of unprocessed logs and chips of eighteen eucalypt species from Australia. Gen. Tech. Rep. FPL-137. Madison, WI: U.S. Department of Agriculture, Forest Service, Forest Products Laboratory. 206 p.

Kliejunas, J.T.; Geils, B.W.; Glaeser, J.M.; Goheen, E.M.; Hennon, P.; Kim, M.-S.; Kope, H.; Stone, J.; Sturrock, R.; Frankel, S.J. 2009. Review of literature on climate change and forest diseases of western North America. Gen. Tech. Rep. PSW-GTR-225. Albany, CA: U.S. Department of Agriculture, Forest Service, Pacific Southwest Research Station. 54 p.

Klinka, K.; Worrall, J.; Skoda, L.; Varga, P. 2000. The distribution and synopsis of ecological and silvical characteristics of tree species of British Columbia's forests. Coquitlam, BC: Canadian Cartographics Ltd. 180 p.

Klopfenstein, N.B.; Kim, M.-S.; Hanna, J.W.; Richardson, B.A.; Lundquist, J.E. 2009a. Approaches to predicting potential impacts of climate change on forest disease: an example with Armillaria root disease. Res. Pap. RMRS-RP-76. Fort Collins, CO: U.S. Department of Agriculture, Forest Service, Rocky Mountain Research Station. 10 p.

Klopfenstein, N.B.; Lundquist, J.E.; Hanna, J.W.; Kim, M.-S.; McDonald, G.I. 2009b. First report of *Armillaria sinapina*, a cause of Armillaria root disease, associated with a variety of forest tree hosts on sites with diverse climates in Alaska. Plant Disease. 93: 111.

Kuhlman, E.G.; Hodges, C.S., Jr.; Froelich, R.C. 1976. Minimizing losses to *Fomes annosus* in the southern United States. Res. Pap. SE-151. Ashville, NC: U.S. Department of Agriculture, Forest Service, Southeastern Forest Experiment Station. 16 p.

Lane, C.R.; Beales, P.A.; Hughes, K.J.D.; Griffin, R.L.; Munro, R.L.; Brasier, C.M.; Webber, J.F. 2003. First outbreak of *Phytophthora ramorum* in England on *Viburnum tinus*. Plant Pathology. 52: 414.

Littlefield, E.W. 1930. Some experiments made with regard to sprouting in two species of wild gooseberry (*Ribes rotundifolium* Michx. and *R. cynosbati* L.). Blister Rust News. 14: 90–104.

Livingston, W.H. 1990. *Armillaria ostoyae* in young spruce plantations. Canadian Journal of Forest Research. 20: 1773–1778.

Logan, J.A.; Powell, J.A. 2001. Ghost forests, global warming, and the mountain pine beetle (Coleoptera: Scolytidae). American Entomologist. 47: 160–172.

Lonsdale, D.; Gibbs, J. 2002. Effect of climate change on fungal diseases of trees. In: Broadmeadow, M.S.J., ed. Climate change: impacts on UK forests. Bull. No. 125. Edinburgh, United Kingdom: UK Forestry Commission: 83–97.

Loomis, R.C.; Tucker, S.; Hofacker, T. 1985. Insect and disease conditions in the United States, 1979–1983. Gen. Tech. Rep. GTR-WO-46. Washington, DC: U.S. Department of Agriculture, Forest Service. [Pages unknown].

Lyon, L.J.; Stickney, P.F. 1976. Early vegetal succession following large northern Rocky Mountain wildfires. In: Tall Timbers fire ecology conference and Intermountain Fire Council and Land Management symposium. Proceedings No. 14. Tallahassee, FL: Tall Timbers Research Station: 335–375.

Magarey, R.; Fowler, G.; Colunga, M.; Smith, B.; Meentemeyer, R. 2008. Climate-host mapping of *Phytophthora ramorum*, causal agent of sudden oak death. In: Frankel, S.J.; Kliejunas, J.T.; Palmieri, K.M., tech. coords. Proceedings of the sudden oak death third science symposium. PSW-GTR-214. Albany, CA: U.S. Department of Agriculture, Forest Service, Pacific Southwest Research Station: 269–275.

Maguire, D.A.; Kanaskie, A.; Johnson, R. 2002. Growth of young Douglas-fir plantations across a gradient of Swiss needle cast severity. Western Journal of Applied Forestry. 17: 86–95.

Mainwaring, D.B.; Maguire, D.A.; Kanaskie, A.; Brandt, J. 2005. Growth responses to commercial thinning in Douglas-fir stands with varying severity of Swiss needle cast in Oregon, USA. Canadian Journal of Forest Research. 35: 2394–2402.

Maloney, P.E.; Kane, S.F.; Jensen, C.E.; Rizzo, D.M. 2002. Epidemiology and ecology of *Phytophthora ramorum* in redwood/tanoak forest ecosystems of the California Coast Range. In: Proceedings of the sudden oak death science symposium, the state of our knowledge. Berkeley, CA: U.S. Department of Agriculture, Forest Service and University of California, Berkeley.

Manter, D.K.; Bond, B.J.; Kavanagh, K.L.; Rosso, P.H.; Filip, G.M. 2000. Pseudothecia of Swiss needle cast fungus, *Phaeocryptopus gaeumannii*, physically block stomata of Douglas fir, reducing CO_2 assimilation. New Phytologist. 148: 481–491.

Manter, D.K.; Reeser, P.W.; Stone, J.K. 2005. A climate-based model for predicting geographic variation in Swiss needle cast severity in the Oregon coast range. Phytopathology. 95: 1256–1265.

Mark, W.R.; Hawksworth, F.G. 1976. Distribution of ponderosa pine dwarf mistletoe (*Arceuthobium vaginatum* subsp. *cryptopodum*) in relation to climatic factors. In: 4th national conference on fire and forest meteorology. [Place of publication unknown]: Society of American Foresters and American Meteorological Society. [Pages unknown].

Marks, G.C.; Smith, I.W.; Cook, I.O. 1989. Spread of *Dothistroma septospora* in plantations of *Pinus radiata* in Victoria between 1979 and 1988. Australian Forestry. 52: 10–19.

Martin, F.N. 2008. Mitochondrial haplotype determination in the oomycete plant pathogen *Phytophthora ramorum*. Current Genetics. 54: 23–34.

McDonald, G.I.; Dekker-Robertson, D.L. 1998. Long-term differential expression of blister rust resistance in western white pine. In: Jalkanen, R., ed. First IUFRO Rusts of forest trees proceedings. Rovaniemi, Finland: The Finnish Forest Research Institute: 285–295.

McDonald, G.I.; Martin, N.E.; Harvey, A.E. 1987. Occurrence of *Armillaria* spp. in forests of the northern Rocky Mountains. Res. Pap. INT-381. Ogden, UT: U.S. Department of Agriculture, Forest Service, Intermountain Research Station. 7 p.

McDonald, G.I.; Richardson, B.A.; Zambino, P.J.; Klopfenstein, N.B.; Kim, M.-S. 2006. *Pedicularis* and *Castilleja* are natural hosts of *Cronartium ribicola* in North America: a first report. Forest Pathology. 36: 73–82.

Merrill, L.M.; Hawksworth, F.G.; Jacobi, W.R. 1987. Frequency and severity of ponderosa pine dwarf mistletoe in relation to habitat type and topography in Colorado. Plant Disease. 71: 342–344.

Mielke, J.L. 1943. White pine blister rust in western North America. Bulletin 52. New Haven, CT: Yale University, School of Forestry. 155 p.

Millar, C.I.; Westfall, R.D.; Delany, D.L. 2005. Limber pine forest mortality event in response to 1990s persistent low precipitation and high minimum temperatures. American Geophysical Union, Fall meeting 2005, abstract No. GC33A-1251. http://adsabs.harvard.edu/abs/2005AGUFMGC33A1251M. (June 2011).

Miller, M. 2000. Fire autecology. Wildland fire in ecosystems: effects of fire on flora. Gen. Tech. Rep. RMRSGTR-42. Ogden, UT: U.S. Department of Agriculture, Forest Service, Rocky Mountain Research Station: 9–34.

Moore, B.; Allard, G. 2008. Climate change impacts on forest health. Working Paper FBS/34E. Rome, Italy: Forestry Department Food and Agriculture Organization of the United Nations. 38 p.

Morrison, D.J. 1981. Armillaria root disease. A guide to disease diagnosis, development and management in British Columbia. Rep. BC-X-203. Victoria, BC: Canadian Forest Service, Pacific Forestry Research Centre. 15 p.

Morrison, D.J.; Chu, D.; Johnson, A.L.S. 1985. Species of *Armillaria* in British Columbia. Canadian Journal of Plant Pathology. 7: 242–246.

Morrison, D.J.; Mallet, K.I. 1996. Silvicultural management of Armillaria root disease in western Canadian forests. Canadian Journal of Plant Pathology. 18: 194–199.

Morrison, D.J.; Pellow, K.W. 1994. Development of Armillaria root disease in a 25-year-old Douglas-fir plantation. In: Johansson, M.; Stenlid, J., eds. Proceedings of the 8th international conference on root and butt rots. Wik, Sweden, and Haikko, Finland: Swedish University of Agricultural Sciences, Uppsala: 560–571.

Morrison, D.J.; Pellow, K.W.; Norris, D.J.; Nemec, A.F.L. 2000. Visible versus actual incidence of Armillaria root disease in juvenile coniferous stands in the southern interior of British Columbia. Canadian Journal of Forest Research. 30: 405–414.

Moss, V.D.; Wellner, C.A. 1953. Aiding blister rust control by silvicultural measures in the western white pine type. Circular 919. Washington, DC: U.S. Department of Agriculture. 32 p.

Mote, P.W.; Parson, E.A.; Hamlet, A.F.; Keeton, W.S.; Lettenmaier, D.; Mantua, N.; Miles, E.L.; Peterson, D.W.; Peterson, D.L.; Slaughter, R.; Snover, A.K. 2003. Preparing for climatic change: the water, salmon, and forests of the Pacific Northwest. Climatic Change. 61: 45–88.

National Research Council [NRC]. 1983. Risk assessment in the federal government: managing the process. Washington, DC: National Academic Press. 191 p.

Neuenschwander, L.F.; Byler, J.W.; Harvey, A.E.; McDonald, G.I.; Ortiz, D.S.; Osborne, H.L.; Snyder, G.C.; Zack, A. 1999. White pine in the American West: a vanishing species—Can we save it? Gen. Tech. Rep. RMRS-GTR-35. Moscow, ID: U.S. Department of Agriculture, Forest Service, Rocky Mountain Research Station. 20 p.

Orr, R.L.; Cohen, S.D.; Griffin, R.L. 1993. Generic nonindigenous pest risk assessment process (for estimating pest risk associated with the introduction of nonindigenous organisms) Riverdale, MD: U.S. Department of Agriculture, Animal and Plant Health Inspection Service (internal report). 40 p.

Otrosina, W.; Garbelotto, M. 2010. *Heterobasidion occidentale* sp. nov. and *Heterobasidion irregulare* nom. nov.: a disposition of North American *Heterobasidion* biological species. Fungal Biology. 114: 16–25.

Patton, R.F. 1997. Red band needle blight. In: Hansen, E.M.; Lewis, K.J., eds. Compendium of conifer diseases. St. Paul, MN: American Phytopathological Society Press: 57–59.

Peterson, G.W. 1966. Penetration and infection of Austrian and ponderosa pine by *Dothistroma pini*. Phytopathology. 56: 894–895.

Peterson, G.W. 1973. Infection of Austrian and ponderosa pines by *Dothistroma pini* in eastern Nebraska. Phytopathology. 63: 1060–1063.

Peterson, G.W. 1982. Dothistroma needle blight of pines. Forest Insect and Disease Leaflet 143. Washington, DC: U.S. Department of Agriculture, Forest Service.

Peterson, G.W.; Walla, J.A. 1978. Development of *Dothistroma pini* upon and within needles of Austrian and ponderosa pine in eastern Nebraska. Phytopathology. 68: 1422–1430.

Peterson, R.S. 1971. Wave years of infection by western gall rust on pine. Plant Disease Reporter. 55: 163–167.

Pojar, J. 2010. A new climate for conservation: nature, carbon, and climate change in British Columbia. Vancouver, BC: West Coast Environmental Law. 100 p. http://www.borealbirds.org/resources/report-pojar-bcconservation.pdf. (June 2010).

Quick, C.R. 1954. Ecology of the Sierra Nevada gooseberry in relation to blister rust control. Circular 937. Washington, DC: U.S. Department of Agriculture. 30 p.

Ray, A.J.; Barsugli, J.J.; Averyt, K.B. 2008. Climate change in Colorado: a synthesis to support water resources management and adaptation. A report by the Western Water Assessment for the Colorado Water Conservation Board. Boulder, CO: Cooperative Institute for Research in Environmental Sciences, Western Water Assessment, University of Colorado at Boulder. http://cwcb. state.co.us/public-information/publications/Documents/ReportsStudies/ ClimateChangeReportFull.pdf. (June 2011).

Reich, R.M.; Mielke, P.W.; Hawksworth, F.G. 1991. Spatial analysis of ponderosa pine trees infected with dwarf mistletoe. Canadian Journal of Forest Research. 21: 1808–1815.

Ribeiro, O.K. 1983. Physiology of asexual sporulation and spore germination in *Phytophthora*. In: Erwin, D.C.; Bartnicki-Garcia, S.; Tsao, P.H., eds. *Phytophthora*, its biology, taxonomy, ecology, and pathology. St. Paul, MN: APS Press: 55–70.

Riker, A.J.; Kouba, T.F.; Henry, B.W. 1947. The influence of temperature and humidity on the development of white pine blister rust on *Ribes* leaves. Phytopathology. 37: 19.

Rizzo D.M.; Garbelotto, M.; Davidson, J.M.; Slaughter, G.W.; Koike, S.T. 2002. *Phytophthora ramorum* as the cause of extensive mortality of *Quercus* spp. and *Lithocarpus densiflorus* in California. Plant Disease. 86: 205–214.

Rizzo, D.M.; Garbelotto, M.; Hansen, E. 2005. *Phytophthora ramorum*: integrative research and management of an emerging pathogen in California and Oregon forests. Annual Review of Phytopathology. 43: 309–335.

Rohrs-Richey, J. 2008. Increased severity of alder canker expected with climate change in Alaska: Can hosts adjust physiology to compensate for disease? Phytopathology. 98: S192.

Runion, G.B. 2003. Climate change and plant pathosystems—future disease prevention starts here. New Phytologist. 159: 531–538.

Sansford, C.E.; Inman, A.J.; Baker, R.; Brasier, C.; Frankel, S.; de Gruyter, J.; Husson, C.; Kehlenbeck, H.; Kessel, G.; Moralejo, E.; Steeghs, M.; Webber, J.; Werres, S. 2009. Report on the risk of entry, establishment, spread and socio-economic loss and environmental impact and the appropriate level of management for *Phytophthora ramorum* for the EU. Deliverable Report 28. Sand Hutton, York, United Kingdom: Forestry Research, Central Science Laboratory. EU Sixth Framework Project, RAPRA. 310 p. http://rapra.csl.gov.uk/RAPRA-PRA_26feb09.pdf. (June 2011).

Sansford, C.E.; Woodhall, J.W. 2007. Datasheet for *Phytophthora ramorum*. PPP 11824. Sand Hutton, York: Central Science Laboratory, Department of Environment, Forestry, and Rural Affairs. 43 p. http://www.suddenoakdeath.org/pdf/pram_PRA_UK.pdf. (June 2011).

Schaberg, P.G.; Hennon, P.E.; D'Amore, D.V.; Hawley, G.J. 2008. Influence of simulated snow cover on the cold tolerance and freezing injury of yellow-cedar seedlings. Global Change Biology. 14: 1–12.

Scharpf, R.F. 1978. Mistletoes. In: Bega, R.V., tech. coord. Diseases of Pacific coast conifers. Agric. Handb. 521. Washington, DC: U.S. Department of Agriculture, Forest Service: 121–141.

Scherm, H.; Ngugi, H.K.; Ojiambo, P.S. 2006. Trends in theoretical plant epidemiology. European Journal of Plant Pathology. 115: 61–73.

Schoeneweiss, D.F. 1975. Predisposition, stress, and plant disease. Annual Review of Phytopathology. 13: 193–211.

Schoeneweiss, D.F. 1981. Infectious diseases of trees associated with water and freezing stress. Journal of Arboriculture. 7: 13–18.

Schultz, D.; Allison, J. 1982. Tree mortality in the Cleveland National Forest. For. Pest Mgmt. Rep. 82-12. San Francisco, CA: U.S. Department of Agriculture, Forest Service, Pacific Southwest Region. 17 p.

Schultz, D.; Kliejunas, J. 1982. A biological evaluation of pine mortality of the San Jacinto Ranger District, San Bernardino National Forest. For. Pest Mgmt. Rep. 82-5. San Francisco, CA: U.S. Department of Agriculture, Forest Service, Pacific Southwest Region. 10 p.

Shain, L.; Franich, R.A. 1981. Induction of Dothistroma blight symptoms with dothistromin. Physiological Plant Pathology. 19: 49–55.

Shaw, C.G., III. 1988. Is *Heterobasidion annosum* poorly adapted to incite disease in cool, wet environments? In: Otrosina, W.J.; Scharpf, R.F., tech. coords. Symposium on research and management of annosus root disease in western North America. Gen. Tech. Rep. PSW-116. Berkeley, CA: U.S. Department of Agriculture, Forest Service, Pacific Southwest Forest and Range Experiment Station: 101–104.

Shaw, C.G., III; Kile, G.A. 1991. Armillaria root disease. Agric. Handb. 691. Washington, DC: U.S. Department of Agriculture, Forest Service. 233 p.

Sheldon, C. 1912. The wilderness of the North Pacific Coast islands: a hunter's experience while searching for wapiti, bears, and caribou on the larger islands of British Columbia and Alaska. New York: Scribner's Sons. 246 p.

Shishkoff, N. 2007. Persistence of *Phytophthora ramorum* in soil mix and roots of nursery ornamentals. Plant Disease. 91: 1245–1249.

Singh, P.; Richardson, J. 1973. Armillaria root rot in seeded and planted areas in Newfoundland. Forestry Chronicle. 49: 180–182.

Smith, M.L.; Bruhn, J.N.; Anderson, J.B. 1992. The fungus *Armillaria bulbosa* is among the largest and oldest living organisms. Nature. 356: 428–431.

Smith, R.S., Jr. 1978. Needle diseases. In: Bega, R.V., tech coord. Diseases of Pacific Coast conifers. Agric. Handb. 521. Washington, DC: U.S. Department of Agriculture, Forest Service: 42–68.

Snyder, C. 2005. Forest health conditions in Alaska—2005. Protection Report R10-PR-5. Juneau, AK: U.S. Department of Agriculture, Forest Service, Forest Health Protection. 92 p.

Spaulding, P. 1922. Investigations of the white-pine blister rust. Bull. 957. Washington, DC: U.S. Department of Agriculture, Forest Service. 100 p.

Spittlehouse, D. 2008. Climate change, impacts, and adaptation scenarios: climate change and forest and range management in British Columbia. Tech. Rep. 45. Victoria, BC: BC Ministry of Forests and Range, Research Branch. 38 p.

Stanosz, G.R.; Trummer, L.M.; Rohrs-Richey, J.K. 2008. Response of *Alnus tenuifolia* to inoculation with *Valsa melanodiscus*. Phytopathology. 98: S150.

Stone, J.K.; Coop, L.B.; Manter, D.K. 2008. Predicting effects of climate change on Swiss needle cast disease severity in Pacific Northwest forests. Canadian Journal of Plant Pathology. 30: 169–176.

Stone, J.K.; Hood, I.A.; Watt, M.S.; Kerrigan, J.L. 2007. Distribution of Swiss needle cast in New Zealand in relation to winter temperature. Australasian Plant Pathology. 36: 445–454.

Sturrock, R.N. 2007. Climate change effects on forest diseases: an overview. In: Jackson, M.B., comp. Proceedings of the 54th annual western international forest disease work conference. Missoula, MT: U.S. Department of Agriculture, Forest Service, Northern Region, Forest Health Protection: 51–55.

Sturrock, R.N.; Frankel, S.J.; Brown, A.; Hennon, P.E.; Kliejunas, J.T.; Lewis, K.J.; Worrall, J.J.; Woods, A.J. 2011. Climate change and forest diseases. Plant Pathology. 60: 133–149.

Tooley, P.W.; Browning, M.; Berner, D. 2008. Recovery of *Phytophthora ramorum* following exposure to temperature extremes. Plant Disease. 92: 431–437.

Tomback, D.F.; Achuff, P. 2010. Blister rust and western forest biodiversity: ecology, values, and outlooks for white pines. Forest Pathology. 40: 186–225.

Towers, B.; Stambaugh, W.J. 1968. The influence of induced moisture stress upon *Fomes annosus* root rot of loblolly pine. Phytopathology. 58: 269–272.

Trummer, L. 2006. Alder canker. In: Snyder, C., ed. Forest health conditions in Alaska—2005. Forest Health Protection report R10-PR-5. Anchorage, AK: U.S. Department of Agriculture, Forest Service, Alaska Region: 52.

Turner, J.; Jennings, P. 2008. Report indicating the limiting and optimal environmental conditions for production, germination and survival of sporangia and zoospores. Deliverable Report 7. Sand Hutton, York, United Kingdom: Forestry Research. On file with: Central Science Laboratory, Department of Environment, Food and Rural Affairs, Sand Hutton, York, YO41 1LZ.

U.S. Department of Agriculture, Forest Service [USDA FS]. 1999. 1999 Alaska insect and disease conditions report. http://forestry.alaska.gov/pdfs/cond_report99-4.pdf. (June 2011).

U.S. Department of Agriculture, Forest Service [USDA FS]. 2003. Climate models predict wetter winters, warmer summers in the West. Science Daily. (November 14). http://www.sciencedaily.com/releases/2003/11/031114072917.htm. (June 2011).

U.S. Department of Agriculture, Forest Service [USDA FS]. 2007. Forest insect and disease conditions in the United States 2006. Washington, DC: Forest Health Protection. 176 p.

U.S. Office of Technology Assessment. 1993. A primer on climate change and natural resources. Preparing for an uncertain climate. Washington, DC: Government Printing Office. [Pages unknown].

Van Arsdel, E.P. 1954. Climatic factors affecting the distribution of the white pine blister rust in Wisconsin. Madison, WI: University of Wisconsin. 105 p. Ph.D dissertation.

Van Arsdel, E.P. 1965. Micrometeorology and plant disease epidemiology. Phytopathology. 55: 945–950.

Van Arsdel, E.P. 1972. Environment in relation to white pine blister rust infection. In: Bingham, R.T.; Hoff, R.J.; McDonald, G.I., eds. Biology of rust resistance in forest trees. Misc. Publ. 1221. Washington, DC: U.S. Department of Agriculture, Forest Service: 479–493.

Van Arsdel, E.P.; Geils, B.W.; Zambino, P.J. 2006. Epidemiology for hazard rating of white pine blister rust. In: Guyon, J.C., comp. 53rd annual western international forest disease work conference. Ogden, UT: U.S. Department of Agriculture, Forest Service, Intermountain Region: 49–64.

Van Arsdel, E.P.; Riker, A.J.; Kouba, T.F.; Suomi, V.E.; Bryson, R.A. 1961. The climatic distribution of blister rust on white pine in Wisconsin. Station Pap. 87. St. Paul, MN: U.S. Department of Agriculture, Forest Service, Lake States Experiment Station. 34 p.

Van Arsdel, E.P.; Riker, A.J.; Patton, R.F. 1956. The effects of temperature and moisture on the spread of white pine blister rust. Phytopathology. 46(6): 307–318.

van der Pas, J.B. 1981. Reduced early growth rates of *Pinus radiata* caused by *Dothistroma pini*. N.Z. Journal of Forest Science. 11: 210–220.

Venette, R.C. 2009. Implication of global climate change on the distribution and activity of *Phytophthora ramorum*. In: McManus, K.A.; Gottschalk, K.W., eds. Proceedings. 20th U.S. Department of Agriculture interagency research forum on invasive species. Gen. Tech. Rep. NRS-P-51. Newtown Square, PA: U.S. Department of Agriculture, Forest Service, Northern Research Station: 58–59. http://www.nrs.fs.fed.us/pubs/gtr/gtr-nrs-p-51papers/33venette-p-51.pdf. (June 2011).

Venette, R.C.; Cohen, S.D. 2006. Potential climatic suitability for establishment of *Phytophthora ramorum* within the contiguous United States. Forest Ecology and Management. 231: 18–26.

Villebonne, D.; Maugard, F. 1999. Rapid development of Dothistroma needle blight (*Scirrhia pini*) on Corsican pine (*Pinus nigra* subsp. *laricio*) in France. La Sante des Forets, Annual Report 1998. Paris: Les Cahiers du DSF 1, DERF: 30–32.

Wargo, P.M.; Harrington, T.C. 1991. Host stress and susceptibility to *Armillaria*. In: Shaw, C.G., III; Kile, G., eds. Armillaria root disease. Agric. Handb. 691. Washington, DC: U.S. Department of Agriculture: 88–101.

Wargo, P.M.; Shaw, C.G., III. 1985. Armillaria root rot: the puzzle is being solved. Plant Disease. 69: 826–832.

Warwell, M.V.; Rehfeldt, G.E.; Crookston, N.L. 2007. Modeling contemporary climate profiles and predicting their response to global warming for whitebark pine (*Pinus albicaulis*). In: Goheen, E.M.; Sniezko, R.A., eds. Whitebark pine: a Pacific Coast perspective. R6-NR-FHP-2007-01. Portland, OR: U.S. Department of Agriculture, Forest Service, Pacific Northwest Region: 139–142.

Watt, M.S.; Kriticos, D.J.; Alcaraz, S.; Brown, A.V.; Leriche, A. 2009. The hosts and potential geographic range of Dothistroma needle blight. Forest Ecology and Management. 257: 1505–1519.

Watt, M.S.; Stone, J.K.; Hood, I.A.; Palmer, D.J. 2010. Predicting the severity of Swiss needle cast on Douglas-fir under current and future climate in New Zealand. Forest Ecology and Management. 260: 2232–2240.

Webber, J.F.; Mullett, M.; Brasier, C.M. 2010. Dieback and mortality of plantation Japanese larch (*Larix kaempferi*) associated with infection by *Phytophthora ramorum*. New Disease Reports. 22: 19.

Weiss, J.; Overpeck, J. 2005. Is the Sonoran Desert losing its cool? Global Change Biology. 11: 2065–2077.

Welsh, C.; Lewis, K.; Woods, A. 2009. The outbreak history of Dothistroma needle blight: an emerging forest disease in northwestern British Columbia, Canada. Canadian Journal of Forest Research. 39: 2505–2519.

Werres, S.; Marwitz, R.; Man In't Veld, W.A.; De Cock, A.W.A.M.; Bonants, P.J.M.; De Weerdt, M.; Themann, K.; Iliev, E.; Baayen, R.P. 2001. *Phytophthora ramorum* sp. nov., a new pathogen on *Rhododendron* and *Viburnum*. Mycological Research. 105: 1155–1165.

Whitney, R.D. 1984. Site variation of *Armillaria mellea* in three Ontario conifers. In: Kile, G.A., ed. Proceedings of the 6th international conference on root and butt rots of forest trees. Melbourne, Victoria: Commonwealth Scientific and Industrial Research Organization: 122–130.

Whitney, R.D. 1988. Armillaria root rot damage in softwood plantations in Ontario. Forestry Chronicle. 64: 345–351.

Williams, R.E.; Marsden, M.A. 1982. Modeling probability of root disease center occurrence in northern Idaho forests. Canadian Journal of Forest Research. 12: 876–882.

Williams, J.W.; Jackson, S.T.; Kutzbach, J.E. 2007. Projected distributions of novel and disappearing climates by 2100 AD. Proceedings of the National Academy of Sciences. 104(14): 5738–5742.

Williams, W.T. 1971. Distribution of three species of dwarf mistletoe on their principal pine hosts in the Colorado Rocky Mountain Front Range. Phytopathology. 61: 1324–1325.

Wilson, J.L.; Tkacz, B.M. 1992. Pinyon ips outbreak in pinyon juniper woodlands in northern Arizona: a case study. Gen. Tech. Rep. RM-218. Fort Collins, CO: U.S. Department of Agriculture, Forest Service, Rocky Mountain Forest and Range Experiment Station: 187–190.

Wood, R.E.; Shuft, M.J.; Schultz, D.E. 1979. An evaluation of tree mortality in Laguna Mountain Recreation Area, Cleveland National Forest. Forest Insect and Disease Mgmt. Rep. 79-1. San Francisco, CA: U.S. Department of Agriculture, Forest Service, Pacific Southwest Region. 22 p.

Woods, A.J. 2003. Species diversity and forest health in northwest British Columbia. Forestry Chronicle. 79(5): 892–897.

Woods, A.; Coates, K.D.; Hamann, A. 2005. Is an unprecedented Dothistroma needle blight epidemic related to climate change? BioScience. 55: 761–769.

Woods, A.J.; Heppner, D.; Kope, H.; Burleigh, J.; Maclauchlan, L. 2010. Forest health and climate change: a British Columbia perspective. Forestry Chronicle. 86: 412–422.

Worrall, J.J. 2009. Dieback and mortality of *Alnus* in the southern Rocky Mountains, USA. Plant Disease. 93(3): 293–298.

Worrall, J. 2010. Forest and shade tree pathology. http://www.forestpathology.org/. (June 2011).

Worrall, J.; Sullivan, K. 2002. Discoloration of ponderosa pine on the San Juan National Forest, 1999–2001. Biological Evaluation R2-02-06. Gunnison, CO: U.S. Department of Agriculture, Forest Service, Rocky Mountain Region, Forest Health Management. 20 p.

Worrall, J.J.; Adams, G.C.; Tharp, S.C. 2010. Summer heat and an epidemic of *Cytospora* canker of *Alnus*. Canadian Journal of Plant Pathology. 32: 376–386.

Zambino, P.J. 2010. Biology and pathology of *Ribes* and their implications for management of white pine blister rust. Forest Pathology. 40: 264–291.

Zeglan, S.; Pronos, J.; Merler, H. 2010. Silvicultural management of white pines in western North America. Forest Pathology. 40: 347–368.

This publication is available online at http://www.fs.fed.us/psw/. You may also order additional copies of it by sending your mailing information in label form through one of the following means. Please specify the publication title and series number.

Fort Collins Service Center

Web site	http://www.fs.fed.us/psw/
Telephone	(970) 498-1392
FAX	(970) 498-1122
E-mail	rschneider@fs.fed.us
Mailing address	Publications Distribution
	Rocky Mountain Research Station
	240 West Prospect Road
	Fort Collins, CO 80526-2098

Pacific Southwest Research Station
800 Buchanan Street
Albany, CA 94710